THE
INFLATION
CRISIS, AND
HOW TO RESOLVE IT

Second Edition

Henry Hazlitt

UNIVERSITY
PRESS OF
AMERICA

LANHAM • NEW YORK • LONDON

Library of Congress Catalog Card Number : 83-10511

Contents

Preface
TO THE SECOND EDITION

When the University Press of America suggested bringing out a new edition of my 1978 book on inflation, my first thought was that this would require bringing all the statistical material up-to-date, and adding a detailed account of what had happened regarding inflation in the five-year period since then. But on further reflection I recognized that all this, though troublesome and time-consuming, would serve little purpose. The new tables and factual statements would soon become out-of-date in turn, just as tomorrow's stock market reports will replace today's, without necessarily teaching any new policy lessons. Economic and monetary lessons are learned not primarily by mistakes but by analysis and basic understanding of the reasons for the mistakes.

I do think it necessary, however, to call attention here to a development of the last two or three years that was not analyzed in my earlier book because it had not occurred up to 1978—at least not to such a dramatic extent. This has been the sudden and sharp rise in real interest rates to a level that brought about a deep recession in business and consequent mass unemployment.

Economists have long pointed out, of course, that in an inflation that has gone on for some time, and is expected to continue, nominal interest rates rise. Lenders want not only a normal rate of return, but a "price premium" to compensate them for the expected fall in the purchasing power of their dollars when they get them back. I discussed this in my 1978 book. (Ch. 17, pp. 121 et seq.)

But the rise in interest rates in the summer of 1982 was much greater than the general expectation of the future inflation rate prevailing at that time would have brought. It was a "real" and not merely "nominal" rise in interest. It made private borrowing almost prohibitive.

5

This was a result of a combination of two factors. The first was a sharp increase in the size of the deficit. The second was the refusal of the Federal Reserve System to monetize the debt to any but a minor extent.

The deficit for the fiscal year 1982, which ended Sept. 30 of that calendar year, was $110.7 billion (compared with an average deficit in the three preceding fiscal years of $48 billion). If the Federal Reserve had bought the government's securities in the open market to an equivalent amount—a frequent practice in the past—this would have led immediately to an accelerated inflation. But it refrained. The result was that the government's enormous borrowings in the open market sent interest rates soaring, and "crowded out" part of the private borrowing that would otherwise have taken place for business expansion or even for continuance of normal production.

As long as deficits of the dimensions of fiscal 1982 continue there is a prospect of either prohibitive interest rates or galloping inflation in the immediate future, depending on how the deficits are financed. We could easily have a combination of both.

Yet this is precisely the policy that is now officially planned. The President's budget message of Jan. 31, 1983 projected a deficit of $188.8 billion for the fiscal year 1984. And even on the assumption that his proposed cutbacks and freezes in spending are adopted, his budget message forecasts deficits of $194 billion in fiscal 1985, $148 billion in 1986, $142 billion in 1987, and $117 billion in 1988. When we consider that we have already had 44 deficits in the 52 years since 1930, that future budget deficits have been chronically underestimated in the past, and that President Reagan himself, at the beginning of his term, projected a balanced budget for the fiscal year 1984, the outlook at the moment of writing this is frightening.

The blame for this is so widespread that it would be a mistake to try to pin it on any particular individual or limited group. Ever since the beginning of the New Deal, successive Congresses and Presidents have treated the immense growth of "social," "entitlement," and other redistributive spending programs as politically untouchable. The immense harm to nearly everyone done by inflation itself has been systematically ignored.

Henry Hazlitt

March, 1983

6

Preface

This book was first planned as a revised edition of my *What You Should Know About Inflation,* first published in 1960. But inflation, not only in the United States but throughout the world, has since then not only continued, but spread and accelerated. The problems it presents, in a score of aspects, have become increasingly grave and urgent, and have called for a wider and deeper analysis.

Therefore this is, in effect, an entirely new book. Only about one-seventh of the material has been taken from the 1960 volume, and even this is revised. The other six-sevenths is new. In order to make the distinction clear for those who may have read the former book, I have divided this volume into two parts. All the material from the older book is included in part one, "Overall View." This does not mean that all of part one appeared there. Chapter 2, for example, presents a forty-year record of inflation instead of the twenty-year record in the previous volume. All of part two, "Close-Ups," is new material. Some of the chapters in this book have appeared in slightly different form as articles in the *Freeman,* though they were written originally for this volume.

What You Should Know About Inflation was essentially a primer. This new volume is more ambitious. In it I have attempted to analyze thoroughly and in depth nearly a score of major problems raised by inflation and chronic fallacies that are in large part responsible for its continuance. So the two parts supplement each other: as suggested by their titles, the first gives an overall view and the second is a series of detailed and close-up examinations.

Because I have taken up these problems and fallacies in separate chapters, and tried to make the discussion of each complete in itself, there is necessarily some repetition. When we take a comprehensive view of each subsidiary problem, we necessarily meet considerations which each shares with the overall problem. Only by this repeated emphasis and varied iteration of certain truths can we hope to make headway against the stubborn sophistries and falsehoods that have led to the persistence of inflationary policies over nearly half a century.

HENRY HAZLITT

February 1978

Part I
Overall View

1

What Inflation Is

No subject is so much discussed today—or so little understood—as inflation. The politicians in Washington talk of it as if it were some horrible visitation from without, over which they had no control—like a flood, a foreign invasion, or a plague. It is something they are always promising to "fight"—if Congress or the people will only give them the "weapons" or "a strong law" to do the job.

Yet the plain truth is that our political leaders have brought on inflation by their own monetary and fiscal policies. They are promising to fight with their right hand the conditions brought on with their left.

What they call inflation is, always and everywhere, primarily caused by an increase in the supply of money and credit. In fact, inflation *is* the increase in the supply of money and credit. If you turn to the *American College Dictionary,* for example, you will find the first definition of inflation given as follows: "Undue *expansion* or increase of the *currency* of a country, esp. by the issuing of paper money not redeemable in specie" (emphasis added).

In recent years, however, the term has come to be used in a radically different sense. This is recognized in the second definition given by the *American College Dictionary:* "A substantial *rise of prices* caused by an undue expansion in paper money or bank credit" (emphasis added). Now obviously a rise of prices *caused* by an expansion of the money supply is not the same thing as the expansion of the money supply itself. A cause or condition is clearly not identical with one of its consequences. The use of the word *inflation* with these two quite different meanings leads to endless confusion.

The word *inflation* originally applied solely to the quantity of money. It meant that the volume of money was *inflated*, blown up, overextended. It is not mere pedantry to insist that the word should be used only in its original meaning. To use it to mean "a rise in prices" is to deflect attention away from the real cause of inflation and the real cure for it.

(However, I have to warn the reader that the word *inflation* is now so commonly used to mean "a rise in prices" that it would be difficult and time-consuming to keep avoiding or refuting it on every occasion. The word has come to be, in fact, almost universally used ambiguously—sometimes in sense one—an increase in money stock—but much more often in sense two—a rise in prices. I have personally found it almost hopelessly difficult to keep from slipping into the same ambiguity. Perhaps the most acceptable compromise, at this late stage, for those of us who keep the distinction in mind, is to remember to use the full phrase *price inflation* when using the word solely in the second sense. I have tried to do this in the following pages, though perhaps not always consistently.)

Let us see what happens under inflation, and why it happens. When the supply of money is increased, people have more money to offer for goods. If the supply of goods does not increase—or does not increase as much as the supply of money—then the prices of goods will go up. Each individual dollar becomes less valuable because there are more dollars. Therefore more of them will be offered against, say, a pair of shoes or a hundred bushels of wheat than before. A "price" is an *exchange ratio* between a dollar and a unit of goods. When people have more dollars, they value each dollar less. Goods then rise in price, not because goods are scarcer than before, but because dollars are more abundant, and thus less valued.

In the old days, governments inflated by clipping and debasing the coinage. Then they found they could inflate cheaper and faster simply by grinding out paper money on a printing press. This is what happened with the French assignats in 1789, and with our own currency during the Revolutionary War. Today the method is a little more indirect. Our government sells its bonds or other IOUs to the banks. In payment, the banks create "deposits" on their books against which the government can draw. A bank in turn may sell its government IOUs to a Federal Reserve bank, which pays for them either by creating a deposit credit or having more Federal Reserve notes printed and paying them out. This is how money is manufactured.

The greater part of the "money supply" of this country is represented not by hand-to-hand currency but by bank deposits which are drawn against by checks. Hence when most economists measure our money supply they add demand deposits (and now frequently, also, time deposits) to currency outside of banks to get the total. The total of money and credit so measured, including time deposits, was $63.3 billion at the end of December 1939, $308.8 billion at the end of December 1963, and $806.5 billion in December 1977. This increase of 1174 percent in the supply of money is overwhelmingly the reason why wholesale prices rose 398 percent in the same period.

Some Qualifications

It is often argued that to attribute inflation solely to an increase in the volume of money is "oversimplification." This is true. Many qualifications have to be kept in mind.

For example, the "money supply" must be thought of as including not only the supply of hand-to-hand currency, but the supply of bank credit—especially in the United States, where most payments are made by check.

It is also an oversimplification to say that the value of an individual dollar depends simply on the *present* supply of dollars outstanding. It depends also on the *expected future* supply of dollars. If most people fear, for example, that the supply of dollars is going to be even greater a year from now than at present, then the present value of the dollar (as measured by its purchasing power) will be lower than the present quantity of dollars would otherwise warrant.

13

Again, the value of any monetary unit, such as the dollar, depends not merely on the *quantity* of dollars but on their *quality*. When a country goes off the gold standard, for example, it means in effect that gold, or the right to get gold, has suddenly turned into mere paper. The value of the monetary unit therefore usually falls immediately, even if there has not yet been any increase in the quantity of money. This is because the people have more faith in gold than they have in the promises or judgment of the government's monetary managers. There is hardly a case on record, in fact, in which departure from the gold standard has not soon been followed by a further increase in bank credit and in printing-press money.

In short, the value of money varies for basically the same reasons as the value of any commodity. Just as the value of a bushel of wheat depends not only on the total present supply of wheat but on the expected future supply and on the quality of the wheat, so the value of a dollar depends on a similar variety of considerations. The value of money, like the value of goods, is not determined by merely mechanical or physical relationships, but primarily by psychological factors which may often be complicated.

In dealing with the causes and cure of inflation, it is one thing to keep in mind real complications; it is quite another to be confused or misled by needless or nonexistent complications.

For example, it is frequently said that the value of the dollar depends not merely on the quantity of dollars but on their "velocity of circulation." Increased velocity of circulation, however, is not a cause of a further fall in the value of the dollar; it is itself one of the consequences of the fear that the value of the dollar is going to fall (or, to put it the other way round, of the belief that the price of goods is going to rise). It is this belief that makes people more eager to exchange dollars for goods. The emphasis by some writers on velocity of circulation is just another example of the error of substituting dubious mechanical for real psychological reasons.

Another blind alley: In answer to those who point out that price inflation is primarily caused by an increase in money and credit, it is contended that the increase in commodity prices often occurs *before* the increase in the money supply. This is true. This is what happened immediately after the outbreak of war in Korea, for example. Strategic raw materials began to go up in price on the fear that they were going to be scarce. Speculators and manufacturers began to buy them to hold for profit or protective inventories. *But to do this they had to borrow more money from the banks.* The rise in prices was accompanied by an equally marked rise in bank loans and deposits. From May 31, 1950, to May 30, 1951, the loans of the country's banks increased by $12 billion. If these increased loans had not been made, and new money (some $6 billion by the end of January 1951) had not been issued against the loans, the rise in prices could not have been sustained. The price rise was made possible, in short, only by an increased supply of money.

Some Popular Fallacies

One of the most stubborn fallacies about inflation is the assumption that it is caused, not by an increase in the quantity of money, but by a "shortage of goods."

It is true that a *rise in prices* (which, as we have seen, should not be identified with inflation) can be caused *either* by an increase in the quantity of money *or* by a shortage of goods—or partly by both. Wheat, for example, may rise in price either because there is an increase in the supply of money or a failure of the wheat crop. But we seldom find, even in conditions of total war, a *general* rise of prices caused by a *general* shortage of goods. Yet so stubborn is the fallacy that inflation is caused by a shortage of goods, that even in the Germany of 1923, after prices had soared hundreds of billions of times, high officials and millions of Germans were blaming the whole thing on a general shortage of goods—at the very moment when foreigners were coming in and buying German goods with gold or their own currencies at prices lower than those of equivalent goods at home.

The rise of prices in the United States since 1939 is constantly being attributed to a shortage of goods. Yet official statistics show that our rate of industrial production in 1977 was six times as great as in 1939. Nor is it any better explanation to say that the rise in prices in wartime is caused by a shortage in *civilian* goods. Even to the extent that civilian goods were really short in time of war, the shortage would not cause any substantial rise in prices if taxes took away as large a percentage of civilian income as rearmament took away of civilian goods.

15

This brings us to another source of confusion. People frequently talk as if a budget deficit were in itself both a necessary and a sufficient cause of inflation. A budget deficit, however, if fully financed by the sale of government bonds paid for out of real savings, need not cause inflation. And even a budget surplus, on the other hand, is not an assurance against inflation. This was shown, for example, in the fiscal year ended June 30, 1951, when there was substantial inflation *in spite of* a budget surplus of $3.5 billion. The same thing happened in spite of budget surpluses in the fiscal years 1956 and 1957. (Since 1957, we have had nothing but mounting federal deficits with the exception of one year—1969—and prices rose in that year.) A budget deficit, in short, is inflationary only to the extent that it causes an increase in the money supply. And inflation can occur even with a budget surplus if there is an increase in the money supply notwithstanding.

The same chain of causation applies to all the so-called "inflationary pressures"—particularly the so-called "wage-price spiral." If it were not preceded, accompanied, or quickly followed by an increase in the supply of money, an increase in wages above the "equilibrium level" would not cause inflation; it would merely cause unemployment. And an increase in prices without an increase of cash in people's pockets would merely cause a falling off in sales. Wage and price rises, in brief, are usually a *consequence* of inflation. They can *cause* it only to the extent that they force an increase in the money supply.

2

Our Forty-Year
Record

A casual reader of the newspapers and of our weekly periodicals might be excused for getting the impression that our American inflation is something that suddenly broke out in the last two or three years. Indeed, most of the editors of these periodicals seem themselves to have that impression. When told that our inflation has been going on for some forty years, their response is usually one of incredulity.

A large number of them do recognize that our inflation is at least nine or ten years old. They could hardly help doing so, because the official figures issued each month of wholesale and consumer prices are stated as a percentage of prices in 1967. Thus the consumer price index for June 1976 was 170.1, 0.5 percent higher than in the preceding month and 5.9 percent higher than in June of the year before. This means that consumer prices were over 70 percent higher than in 1967, a shocking increase for a nine-year period. The annual increases in consumer prices ranged from 3.38 percent between 1971 and 1972 to more than 11 percent between 1973 and 1974. The overall tendency for the period was for an accelerating rate. The purchasing power of the dollar at the end of the period was equivalent to only about fifty-seven cents compared with just nine years before.

But the inflation may be dated from as early as 1933. It was in March of that year that the United States went off the gold standard. And it was in January 1934 that the new irredeemable dollar was devalued to 59.06 percent of the weight in gold into which it had previously been convertible. By 1934, the average of wholesale prices had increased 14 percent over 1933; and by 1937, 31 percent.

But consumer prices in 1933 were almost 25 percent below those of 1929. Nearly everybody at the time wanted to see them restored toward that level. So it may be regarded as unfair to begin our inflationary count with that year. Yet even when we turn to a table beginning in 1940, we find that consumer prices as of 1976 were 314 percent higher than then, and that the 1976 dollar had a purchasing power of only twenty-four cents compared with the 1940 dollar.

These results are presented herewith for each year in two tables and three charts. I am indebted to the American Institute for Economic Research at Great Barrington, Massachusetts, for compiling the tables and drawing the charts at my request.

The figures tell their own story, but there are one or two details that deserve special notice. In the thirty-six-year period the nation's money stock has increased about thirteen times, yet consumer prices have increased only a little more than four times. Even in the last nine of those years the money stock increased 119 percent and consumer prices only 74 percent. This is not what the crude quantity theory of money would have predicted, but there are three broad explanations.

First, measuring the increase in the stock of money and credit is to some extent an arbitrary procedure. Some monetary economists prefer to measure it in terms of what is called M_1. This is the amount of currency outside the banks plus demand deposits of commercial banks. The accompanying tables measure the money stock in terms of M_2, which is the amount of currency outside the banks plus both the demand and time deposits of commercial banks. M_1, in other words, measures merely the more active media of purchase, while M_2 includes some of the less active. I have used it because most individuals and corporations who hold time deposits tend to think of them as ready cash when they are considering what purchases they can afford to make in the immediate or near future. But in recent years time deposits have grown at a much faster rate than demand deposits. So if one uses M_2 as one's measuring stick, one gets a much faster rate of increase in the

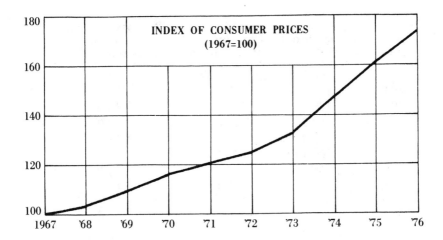

INDEX OF CONSUMER PRICES
(1967=100)

monetary stock than by using M_1. (The latter has increased only eight times since 1940.)

Second, one very important reason why prices have not gone up as fast as the monetary stock is that both overall production and production per capita have risen steadily almost year by year. With the constant increase in capital investment—in the number, quality, and efficiency of machines—both overall productivity and productivity per worker have risen, which means that real costs of production have gone down.

The third explanation has to do with subjective reactions to in-

Year	Money Stock (M_2)	Consumer Price Index	Purchasing Power of the Consumer Dollar
1967	100.0	100.0	100.0
1968	108.9	104.2	96.0
1969	116.2	109.8	91.1
1970	121.0	116.3	86.0
1971	135.0	121.2	82.5
1972	149.3	125.3	79.8
1973	163.6	133.1	75.1
1974	177.4	147.7	67.6
1975	191.0	161.2	62.0
1976	218.7★	173.9★	57.5★

★ Estimated from data through June.

19

Year	Money Stock (M₂)	Consummer Price Index	Purchasing Power of the Consumer Dollar
1940	100.0	100.0	100.0
1941	113.2	105.1	95.1
1942	128.9	116.4	85.9
1943	162.9	123.6	80.9
1944	193.5	125.6	79.6
1945	229.4	128.5	77.8
1946	251.3	139.3	71.7
1947	264.5	159.4	62.7
1948	268.3	171.7	58.2
1949	267.2	170.1	58.8
1950	273.2	171.7	58.2
1951	283.3	185.5	53.9
1952	298.7	189.5	52.7
1953	310.1	191.0	52.4
1954	321.0	191.8	52.1
1955	332.8	191.2	52.3
1956	338.6	194.1	51.5
1957	347.5	200.8	49.8
1958	364.3	206.4	48.5
1959	381.3	207.6	48.2
1960	385.1	211.3	47.3
1961	405.3	213.5	46.8
1962	428.7	216.0	46.3
1963	456.4	218.6	45.7
1964	485.0	221.5	45.1
1965	523.9	225.2	44.4
1966	564.6	231.8	43.1
1967	607.9	238.3	42.0
1968	662.2	248.4	40.3
1969	706.3	261.7	38.2
1970	735.4	277.3	36.1
1971	820.8	288.9	34.6
1972	907.4	298.6	33.5
1973	994.8	317.2	31.6
1974	1,078.5	352.5	28.4
1975	1,160.9	384.2	26.0
1976	1,329.2★	414.3★	24.1★

★ Estimated from data through June.

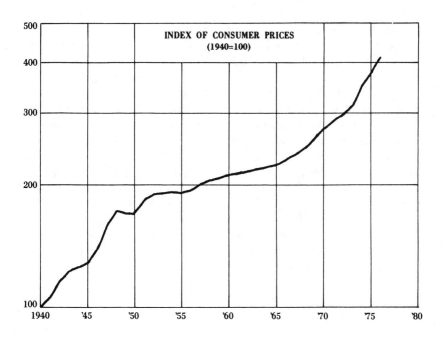

INDEX OF CONSUMER PRICES
(1940=100)

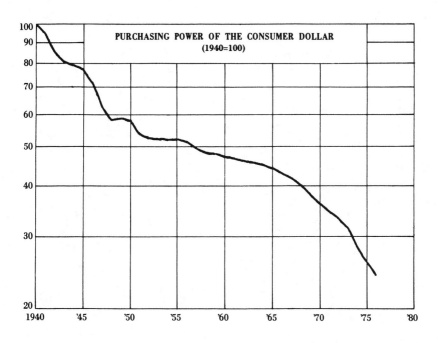

PURCHASING POWER OF THE CONSUMER DOLLAR
(1940=100)

21

creases in the money stock. Statistical comparisons in numerous countries and inflations have shown that, when an inflation is in its early stages or has been comparatively mild, prices tend not to rise as fast as the money stock is increased. The fundamental reason is that most people regard the inflation as an accidental or unplanned occurrence not likely to be continued or repeated. When an inflation is continued or accelerated, however, this opinion can change, and change suddenly and dramatically. The result is that prices start to rise much faster than the stock of money is increased.

The great danger today is that what has been happening since 1939—to prices as compared with the rate of money issue—may have given a false sense of security to our official monetary managers as well as to most commentators in the press. The enormous increase in the American money stock over the past thirty-five to forty years must be regarded as a potential time bomb. It is too late for continued complacency.

3

The Fallacy of "Cost-Push"

In chapter 1, I declared that inflation, always and everywhere, is primarily caused by an increase in the supply of money and credit. There is nothing peculiar or particularly original about this statement. It corresponds closely, in fact, with "orthodox" doctrine. It is supported overwhelmingly by theory, experience, and statistics.

But this simple explanation meets with considerable resistance. Politicians deny or ignore it, because it places responsibility for inflation squarely on their own policies. Few of the academic economists are helpful. Most of them attribute present inflation to a complicated and disparate assortment of factors and "pressures." Labor leaders vaguely attribute inflation to the "greed" or "exorbitant profits" of manufacturers. And most businessmen have been similarly eager to pass the buck. The retailer throws the blame for higher prices on the exactions of the wholesaler, the wholesaler on the manufacturer, and the manufacturer on the raw-material supplier and on labor costs.

This last view is still widespread. Few manufacturers are students of money and banking; the total supply of currency and bank deposits is something that seems highly abstract to most of them and remote from their immediate experience. As one of them once wrote to me: "The thing that increases prices is costs."

What he did not seem to realize is that *cost* is simply another name for a price. One of the consequences of the division of labor is that everybody's price is somebody else's monetary cost, and vice versa. The price of pig iron is the steelmaker's cost. The steelmaker's price is the automobile manufacturer's cost. The automobile manufacturer's price is the doctor's or the taxicab-operating company's cost. And so on. Nearly all costs, it is true, ultimately resolve themselves into salaries or wages. But weekly salaries or hourly wages are the "price" that most of us get for our services.

Now inflation, which is an increase in the supply of money, lowers the value of the monetary unit. This is another way of saying that it raises both prices and costs. And costs do not necessarily go up sooner than prices do. Ham may go up before hogs, and hogs before corn. It is a mistake to conclude, with the old Ricardian economists, that prices are determined by costs of production. It would be just as true to say that costs of production are determined by prices. What hog raisers can afford to bid for corn, for example, depends on the price they are getting for hogs.

In the short run, both prices and costs are determined by the relationships of supply and demand—including, of course, the supply of money as well as goods. It is true that in the long run there is a constant tendency for prices to equal marginal costs of production. This is because, though what a thing *has* cost cannot determine its price, what it *now* costs or is *expected* to cost will determine how much of it will be made.

If these relationships were better understood, fewer editorial writers would attribute inflation to the so-called wage-price spiral. In itself, a wage boost (above the "equilibrium" level) does not lead to inflation but to unemployment. The wage boost can, of course (and under present political pressures usually does), lead to more inflation *indirectly* by leading the government monetary authorities to increase the money supply to make the wage boost payable. But it is the increase in the money supply that causes the inflation. Not until we clearly recognize this will we know how to bring inflation to a halt.

For years we have been talking about the inflationary wage-price spiral. But Washington (by which is meant both the majority in Congress and officials in the executive branch) talks about it for the most part as if it were some dreadful visitation from without, some uncontrollable act of nature, rather than something brought about by its own policies.

Let us see just how those policies, over the last forty-six years, have produced the wage-price spiral. First of all, under a series of laws beginning most notably with the Norris–La Guardia Act of 1932, followed by the Wagner Act and by its later modification, the Taft-Hartley Act, it was decided that labor troubles developed chiefly because there was not enough unionization and because unions were not strong enough.

The federal government was in effect put into the union-organizing business. It compelled employers to deal exclusively with the unions thus quasi-officially set up, regardless of how unreasonable the demands of these unions might turn out to be. Though illegalizing all efforts to deny employment to workers who joined unions, the government explicitly legalized arrangements to deny employment to workers who did not join unions. (In Section 14[b], however, the Taft-Hartley Act did allow any individual state to nullify such a compulsory arrangement within its own borders by enacting special legislation.)

But worst of all, the unions and union members were given a privilege not granted to any other associations or individuals—the power of private coercion and intimidation. The Norris–La Guardia Act in effect prevented either employers or nonunion employees from going to the federal courts for immediate relief from irreparable injury. The government refuses, contrary to legal practice in every other field, to hold a union liable for the acts of its agents. It tolerates mass picketing, which is intimidating and coercive, preventing employers from offering to other workers the jobs abandoned by strikers, and preventing other workers from applying for such jobs. And then officials are astonished and indignant when these special privileges, against which they provide no effective legal protection, are "abused."

The inevitable result of these laws is that there are built up huge unions with the power to bring basic national industries to a halt overnight. And when they have done this, there seems to be no way of getting an industry started again except by giving in to the demands of the union leaders who have called the strike.

This accounts for the upward push on money wage-rates. But it does not account for the inflationary spiral. The effect of pushing wage rates above the level of marginal labor productivity, taken by itself, would simply be to create unemployment. But as F. A. Hayek has put it: "Since it has become the generally accepted doctrine that it is the duty of the monetary authorities to provide enough credit to secure full employment, whatever the wage level, and this duty has in fact been imposed upon the monetary authorities by statute, the power of the unions to push up money wages cannot but lead to continuous, progressive inflation."

Soon or late our federal lawmakers and administrators must face up to the labor-union-boss dictatorship and the wage-price spiral that their own laws and actions have created. But they refuse to do this when each new crisis arises. When, for example, a nationwide steel strike is prolonged, they become panicky. They seek to settle it by the only means that seem possible to them—by giving in once more to union demands, by granting still another wage increase and setting off a new upward wage-price spiral.

Politicians demand that the president appoint a "fact-finding" board to "recommend," i.e., to impose, in effect, compulsory arbitration that would compel the employers to grant another increase to employees. Thus one government intervention begets a further government intervention. Because government has failed in its primary task—that of preventing private coercion—politicians ask, in effect, for price and wage fixing; and we are driven toward totalitarian controls.

4

False Remedy:
Price Fixing

As long as we are plagued by false theories of what causes inflation, we will be plagued by false remedies. Those who ascribe inflation primarily to a shortage of goods, for example, are fond of saying that "the answer to inflation is production." But this is at best a half-truth. It is impossible to bring prices down by increasing production if the money supply is being increased even faster.

The worst of all false remedies for inflation is price-and-wage fixing. If more money is put into circulation, while prices are held down, most people will be left with unused cash balances seeking goods. The final result, barring a like increase in production, must be higher prices.

There are broadly two kinds of price fixing—"selective" and "overall." With selective price fixing the government tries to hold down prices merely of a few strategic war materials or a few necessaries of life. But then the profit margin in producing these things becomes lower than the profit margin in producing other things, including luxuries. So selective price fixing quickly brings about a shortage of the very things whose production the government is most eager to encourage. Then bureaucrats turn to the specious idea of an overall freeze. They talk (in the event of a war) of holding

27

or returning to the prices and wages that existed on the day before war broke out. But the price level and the infinitely complex price and wage interrelationships of that day were the result of the state of supply and demand on that day. And supply and demand seldom remain the same, even for the same commodity, for two days running, even without major changes in the money supply.

In the administration of Franklin D. Roosevelt, the heads of the National Recovery Administration, engaged in overall price control, were asked by a congressional committee how many prices they were fixing. A day or two later they brought in an estimate that there were some 9 million different prices in the United States. Still later they withdrew that estimate as too low. But on the modest estimate of 9 million different prices there are more than *40 trillion* interrelationships of these prices; and a change in one price always has repercussions on a whole network of other prices. The prices and price relationships on the day before the unexpected outbreak of a war, say, are presumably those roughly calculated to encourage a maximum balanced production of *peacetime* goods. They are obviously the wrong prices and price relationships to encourage the maximum production of *war* goods. Moreover, the price pattern of a given day always embodies many misjudgments and "inequities." No single mind, and no bureaucracy, has wisdom and knowledge enough to correct these. Every time a bureaucrat tries to correct one price or wage maladjustment or "inequity" he creates a score of new ones. And there is no precise standard that any two people seem able to agree on for measuring the economic "inequities" of a particular case.

Coercive price fixing would be an insoluble problem, in short, even if those in charge of it were the best-informed economists, statisticians, and businessmen in the country, and even if they acted with the most conscientious impartiality. But they are in fact subjected to tremendous pressures by the organized pressure groups. Those in power soon find that price and wage control is a tremendous weapon with which to curry political favor or to punish opposition. That is why "parity" formulas are applied to farm prices and escalator clauses to wage rates, while industrial prices and dwelling rents are penalized.

Another evil of price control is that, although it is always put into effect in the name of an alleged emergency, it creates powerful vested interests and habits of mind which prolong it or tend to make it permanent. Outstanding examples of this are rent control and exchange control. Price control is the major step toward a fully regimented, or "planned," economy. It causes people to regard it as a matter of course that the government should intervene in every economic transaction.

But finally, and worst of all from the standpoint of inflation, price control diverts attention away from the only real cause of price inflation—the increase in the quantity of money and credit. Hence it prolongs and intensifies the very inflation it was ostensibly designed to cure.

5

What "Monetary Management" Means

Ever since the end of World War II, the public in nearly every country has been told that the gold standard is out of date, and what is needed in its place is "monetary management" by the experts. It is interesting to notice what some of the consequences of this have been.

When Sir Stafford Cripps, then chancellor of the exchequer, announced the devaluation of the British pound from $4.03 to $2.80 on September 18, 1949, Winston Churchill pointed out that Cripps had previously denied any such possibility no fewer than nine times. A United Press dispatch of September 18 listed nine such occasions. A haphazard search on my own part uncovered three more—on September 22 and 28, 1948, and April 30, 1949. Incorporating these in the UP list, we get the following record of denials:

January 26, 1948—"No alteration in the value of sterling is contemplated by the British Government following the devaluation of the franc."

March 4, 1948—A reported plan to devalue the pound is "complete nonsense."

May 6, 1948—"The government has no intention of embarking on a program to devalue the pound."

September 22, 1948—"There will be no devaluation of the pound sterling."

September 28, 1948—The government has "no idea whatever" of devaluing the pound sterling. Devaluation would "increase the price of our imports and decrease the price of exports, which is exactly the opposite of what we are trying to accomplish."

October 5, 1948—"Devaluation is neither advisable nor even possible in present conditions."

December 31, 1948—"No one need fear devaluation of our currency in any circumstances."

April 30, 1949—"Sterling revaluation is neither necessary nor will it take place."

June 28, 1949—"There has been no pressure on me by America to devalue the pound."

July 6, 1949—"The government has not the slightest intention of devaluing the pound."

July 14, 1949—"No suggestion was made at the conference [with Snyder and Abbott] . . . that sterling be devalued. And that, I hope, is that."

September 6, 1949—"I will stick to the . . . statement I made [July 14] in the House of Commons."

In brief, Sir Stafford emphatically denied at least a dozen times that he would do what he did. The excuse has been made for him that naturally he could not afford to admit any such intention in advance because no one would then have accepted sterling at $4.03. This "defense" amounts to saying that unless the government had lied it could not have successfully deceived the buyers of British goods and the holders of sterling.

This is what *devaluation* means. It is a confession of bankruptcy. To announce that IOUs hitherto guaranteed to be worth $4.03 are in fact worth only $2.80 is to tell your creditors that their old claims on you are now worth no more than seventy cents on the dollar.

When a private individual announces bankruptcy, he is thought to be disgraced. When a government does so, it acts as if it had brought off a brilliant coup. This is what our own government did in 1933, and again in August 1971, when it jauntily repudiated its promises to redeem its currency in gold. Here is how the *London Bankers' Magazine* described the 1949 devaluation of the pound by the British Government: "The political technique for dealing with these issues has worn thin. It consists of strenuous, even vicious repudiation beforehand of any notion of revaluation. It insists that the move would be ineffective and utters portentous warning about the dangers. When the unthinkable happens the public is slapped on the back and congratulated on the best piece of luck it has encountered for years."

This is what governments have now been doing for two generations. This is what "monetary management" really amounts to. In practice it is merely a high-sounding euphemism for continuous currency debasement. It consists of constant lying in order to support constant swindling. Instead of automatic currencies based on gold, people are forced to take managed currencies based on guile. Instead of precious metals they hold paper promises whose value falls with every bureaucratic whim. And they are suavely assured that only hopelessly antiquated minds dream of returning to truth and honesty and solvency and gold.

6

Uncle Sam: Swindler?

Fifty years ago H. G. Wells published a minor propagandistic novel called *The Open Conspiracy*. I've forgotten now exactly what that open conspiracy was, but the description seems to fit with peculiar aptness something that is happening in the United States today. Our politicians, and most of our commentators, seem to be engaged in an open conspiracy not to pay the national debt—certainly not in dollars of the same purchasing power as those that were borrowed, and apparently not even in dollars of the present purchasing power.

There is of course no explicit avowal of this intention. The conspiracy is, rather, a conspiracy of silence. Very few of us even mention the problem of substantially reducing the national debt. The most that even the conservatives dare to ask for is that we stop piling up deficits so that we do not have to increase the debt and raise the debt ceiling still further. But anyone with a serious intention of eventually paying off the national debt would have to advocate overbalancing the budget, year in, year out, by a sizable annual sum.

Today one never sees nor hears a serious discussion of this problem. We see hundreds of articles and hear hundreds of speeches in which we are told how we can or should increase federal expenditures or federal tax revenues in proportion to the increase in our "gross national product." But I have yet to see an article that discusses how the government could begin and increase an annual repayment of the debt in proportion to the increase in our gross national product.

When we look at the dimensions the problem has now assumed, it is not difficult to understand the somber silence about it. If someone were to propose that the debt be paid off at an annual rate of $1 billion a year, he would have to face the fact that at that rate it would take more than seven centuries to get rid of it. Yet $1 billion a year is even now no trivial sum. Republican administrations, after World War I, did succeed in maintaining something close to such a steady annual rate of reduction between 1919 and 1930; but they were under continual fire for such a "deflationary" policy. Because of similar deflationary fears, who would dare suggest, say, $7 billion a year?

One suspects that there is at the back of the minds of many of the politicians and commentators who sense the dimensions of the problem an unavowed belief or wish. This is that a continuance of inflation will scale down the real burden of the debt in relation to the national income by a constant shrinkage in the value of the dollar, so reducing the problem to "manageable proportions." Such a policy would be indignantly disavowed. But this is precisely what our reckless spending is leading to. On the debt contracted forty years ago we are paying interest and principal in twenty-three-cent dollars. Are our politicians hoping to swindle government creditors by paying them off in dollars forty years from now at less than a quarter of the purchasing power of the dollar today?

This trick, alas, has a long and inglorious history. In 1776 Adam Smith was already writing in his *Wealth of Nations*:

> When national debts have once been accumulated to a certain degree, there is scarce, I believe, a single instance of their having been fairly and completely paid. The liberation of the public revenue, if it has been brought about at all, has always been brought about by a bankruptcy; sometimes by an avowed one, but always by a real one, though frequently by a pretended payment [i.e., payment in an inflated or depreciated monetary unit]. . . . The honor of a state is surely very poorly

provided for, when, in order to cover the disgrace of a real bankruptcy, it has recourse to a juggling trick of this kind, so easily seen through, and at the same time so extremely pernicious.

Our government is not forced to resort, once more, to such a "juggling trick." It is not too late for it to face its responsibilities now, and to adopt a long-term program that would eventually pay off its creditors with at least the present twenty-three-cent dollar, without plunging us further into inflation or deflation.

7

Why Gold

Seventy years ago, before the outbreak of the First World War, practically every economist of repute supported the gold standard. Most of the merits of that standard were clearly recognized. It was, for one thing, international. When the currency unit of nearly every major country was defined as a specified weight of gold (previous to 1934 the American dollar, for example, was defined as 23.22 grains of fine gold), every such currency unit bore a fixed relation to every other currency unit of the same kind. It was convertible at that fixed ratio, on demand, to any amount, and by anybody who held it, into any other gold currency unit. The result was in effect an international currency system. Gold was the international medium of exchange.

This international gold standard was the chief safeguard against tampering with the currency on the part of politicians and bureaucrats. It was the chief safeguard against domestic inflation. When credit inflation did occur, it produced a quick sequence of results. Domestic prices rose. This encouraged imports and discouraged exports. The balance of trade (or payments) shifted "against" the inflating country. Gold started to flow out. This caused a contraction of the bank credit based on the gold, and brought the inflation to a halt.

Usually, in fact, the chain of consequences was shorter, quicker, and more direct. As soon as foreign bankers and exchange dealers even suspected the existence of inflation in a given country, the exchange rate for that country's currency fell "below the gold point." Gold started to flow out. Then the central-bank managers of the country that was losing gold raised the discount rate. The effect was not merely to halt credit expansion at home, but to draw funds from abroad from lenders who wanted to take advantage of the higher short-term interest rates. The gold flow was stopped or reversed.

Thus so long as the gold standard was resolutely maintained, a whole set of related benefits ensued. Domestic currency tampering and anything more than a relatively moderate inflation were impossible. As gold convertibility had to be maintained at all times, confidence had to be maintained not only through every year but every day. Unsound monetary and economic policies, or even serious proposals of unsound policies, were immediately reflected in exchange rates and in gold movements. The unsound policies or proposals, therefore, had to be quickly moderated or abandoned.

Because there was a fixed and dependable exchange ratio as well as free convertibility between one currency unit and another, international trade, lending, and investment were undertaken freely and with confidence. And, finally, the international gold standard established (apart from differences caused by shipping costs and tariffs) uniform world prices for transportable commodities— wheat, coffee, sugar, cotton, wool, lead, copper, silver, etc.

It has become fashionable to say that in a major crisis, such as war, the gold standard "breaks down." But except to the extent that the citizens of a country fear invasion, conquest, and physical seizure of their gold by the enemy, this is an untrue description of what happens. It is not that the gold standard breaks down, but that it is deliberately abandoned. What the citizens of a country really fear in such crises is inflation by their own monetary managers, or seizure of their gold by their own bureaucrats. This inflation or seizure is not "inevitable" in wartime; it is the result of policy.

It is precisely the merits of the international gold standard which the world's money managers and bureaucrats decry. They do not want to be prevented from inflating whenever they see fit to inflate. They do not want their domestic economy and prices to be tied into the world economy and world prices. They want to be free to manipulate their own domestic price level. They want to pursue purely nationalistic policies (at the expense or imagined expense of other countries), and their pretenses to "internationalism" are a pious fraud.

8

The Cure for Inflation

The cure for inflation, like most cures, consists chiefly in removal of the cause. The cause of price inflation is the increase of money and credit. The cure is to stop increasing money and credit. The cure for inflation, in brief, is to stop inflating. It is as simple as that.

Although simple in principle, this cure often involves complex and disagreeable decisions on detail. Let us begin with the federal budget. It is next to impossible to avoid inflation with a continuing heavy deficit. That deficit is almost certain to be financed by inflationary means—i.e., by directly or indirectly printing more money. Huge government expenditures are not in themselves inflationary—provided they are made wholly out of tax receipts, or out of borrowing paid for wholly out of real savings. But the difficulties in either of these methods of payment, once expenditures have passed a certain point, are so great that there is almost inevitably a resort to the printing press.

Moreover, although huge expenditures wholly met out of huge taxes are not necessarily *inflationary,* they inevitably reduce and disrupt production, and undermine any free enterprise system. The remedy for huge governmental expenditures is therefore not equally huge taxes, but a halt to reckless spending.

On the monetary side, the Treasury and the Federal Reserve

System must stop creating artificially cheap money; that is, they must stop arbitrarily holding down interest rates. The Federal Reserve must not return to the former policy of buying at par the government's own bonds. When interest rates are held artifically low, they encourage an increase in borrowing. This leads to an increase in the money and credit supply. The process works both ways—for it is necessary to increase the money and credit supply in order to keep interest rates artificially low. That is why a "cheap money" policy and a government-bond-support policy are simply two ways of describing the same thing. When the Federal Reserve banks buy government notes or bonds in the open market, they pay for them, directly or indirectly, by creating money. This is what is known as "monetizing" the public debt. Inflation goes on as long as this goes on.

The world will never work itself, and keep itself, out of the present inflationary era until it returns to a full gold standard. The classical gold standard provided a practically automatic check on excessive internal credit expansion. That is why the bureaucrats abandoned it. In addition to being a safeguard against inflation, it was the only system that ever provided the world with the equivalent of an international currency.

The first question to be asked today is not *how* can we stop inflation, but do we really *want* to? For one of the effects of inflation is to bring about a redistribution of wealth and income. In its early stages (until it reaches the point where it grossly distorts and undermines production itself) it benefits some groups at the expense of others. The first groups acquire a vested interest in maintaining inflation. Too many of us continue under the delusion that we can beat the game—that we can increase our own incomes faster than our living costs. So there is a great deal of hypocrisy in the outcry against inflation. Many of us are shouting in effect: "Hold down everybody's price and income except my own."

Governments are the worst offenders in this hypocrisy. At the same time as they profess to be "fighting inflation" they follow a so-called full-employment policy. As one advocate of inflation once put it in the *London Economist:* "Inflation is nine-tenths of *any* full employment policy."

What he forgot to add is that inflation must always end in a crisis and a slump, and that worse than the slump itself may be the public delusion that the slump has been caused, not by the previous inflation, but by the inherent defects of a free market.

Inflation, to sum up, is the increase in the volume of money and bank credit in relation to the volume of goods. It is harmful because it depreciates the value of the monetary unit, raises everybody's cost of living, imposes what is in effect a tax on the poorest (without exemptions) at as high a rate as the tax on the richest, wipes out the value of past savings, discourages future savings, redistributes wealth and income wantonly, encourages and rewards speculation and gambling at the expense of thrift and work, undermines confidence in the justice of a free enterprise system, and corrupts public and private morals.

But it is never inevitable. We can always stop it overnight, if we have the sincere will to do so.

Part II
Close-Ups

9

What Spending and Deficits Do

The direct cause of price inflation is the issuance of an excessive amount of paper money. The most frequent cause of the issuance of too much paper money is a government budget deficit.

The majority of economists have long recognized this, but the majority of politicians have studiously ignored it. One result, in this age of inflation, is that economists have tended to put too much emphasis on the evils of deficits as such and too little emphasis on the evils of excessive government spending, whether the budget is balanced or not.

So it is desirable to begin with the question, What is the effect of government spending on the economy—even if it is wholly covered by tax revenues?

The economic effect of government spending depends on what the spending is for, compared with what the private spending it displaces would be for. To the extent that the government uses its tax-raised money to provide more urgent services for the community than the taxpayers themselves otherwise would or could have provided, the government spending is beneficial to the community. To the extent that the government provides policemen and judges to prevent or mitigate force, theft, and fraud, it protects and encourages production and welfare. The same applies, up to a certain point, to what the government pays out to provide armies and armament against foreign aggression. It applies also to the provision by city governments of sidewalks, streets, and sewers, and to the provision by states of roads, parkways, and bridges.

But government expenditure even on necessary types of service may easily become excessive. Sometimes it may be difficult to measure exactly where the point of excess begins. It is to be hoped, for example, that armies and armament may never need to be used, but it does not follow that providing them is mere waste. They are a form of insurance premium, and in this world of nuclear warfare and incendiary slogans it is not easy to say how large a premium is enough. The exigencies of politicians seeking reelection, of course, may very quickly lead to unneeded roads and other public works.

Waste in government spending in other directions can soon become flagrant. The money spent on various forms of relief, now called "social welfare," is more responsible for the spending explosion of the U.S. government than any other type of outlay. In fiscal year 1927, when total expenditures of the federal government were $2.9 billion, a negligible percentage of that amount went for so-called welfare. In fiscal 1977, when total expenditures rose to $401.9 billion—139 times as much—welfare spending alone (education, social services, Medicaid, Medicare, Social Security, veterans benefits, etc.) came to $221 billion, or more than half the total. The net effect of this spending is to reduce production, because most of it taxes the productive to support the unproductive.

As to the effect of the taxes levied to pay for the spending, all taxation must discourage production to some extent, directly or indirectly. Either it puts a direct penalty on the earning of income, or it forces producers to raise their prices and so diminish their sales, or it discourages investment, or it reduces the savings available for investment; or it does all of these.

Some forms of taxation have more harmful effects on production than others. Perhaps the worst is heavy taxation of corporate earnings. This discourages business and output; it reduces the employment that the politicians profess to be their primary concern; and it prevents the capital formation that is so necessary to increase real productivity, real income, real wages, real welfare. Almost as harmful to incentives and to capital formation is progressive personal income taxation. And the higher the level of any form of taxation, the greater the damage it does.

Let us consider government spending in more detail. The greater the amount of government spending, the more it depresses the economy. In so far as it is a substitute for private spending, it does nothing to "stimulate" the economy. It merely directs labor and capital into the production of less necessary goods or services at the expense of more necessary goods or services. It leads to mal-production. It tends to direct funds out of profitable capital investment and into immediate consumption. And most welfare spending, to repeat, tends to support the unproductive at the expense of the productive.

But more important, the higher the level of government spending, the higher the level of taxation. And the higher the level of taxation, the more it discourages, distorts, and disrupts production. It does this much more than proportionately. A one percent sales tax, personal income tax, or corporation tax would do very little to discourage production, but a 50 percent rate can be seriously disruptive. Just as each additional fixed increment of income will tend to have a diminishing marginal value to the receiver, so each additional *subtraction* from his income will mean a more than proportional deprivation and disincentive. The adjective *progressive* usually carries an approbatory connotation, but an income tax can appropriately be called progressive only in the sense that a disease can be called progressive. So far as its effect on incentives and production are concerned, such a tax is increasingly *retrogressive,* or *repressive.*

Though, broadly speaking, only a budget deficit tends to lead to inflation, the recogntion of this truth has led to a serious underestimation of the harmfulness of an exorbitant level of total government spending. While a budget balanced at a level of $100 billion for both spending and tax revenues may be acceptable (at, say, 1978's level of national income and dollar purchasing power), a budget balanced at a level above $400 billion may in the long run prove ruinous. In the same way, a deficit of $60 billion at a $400 billion level of spending is far more ominous than a deficit of the same size at a spending level of $200 billion.

An exorbitant spending level, in sum, can be as bad as or worse than a huge deficit. Everything depends on their relative size, and on their combined size compared with the national income.

How to Reduce a Deficit

Let us look first at the effect of a deficit. That effect will depend in large part on how the deficit is financed. Of course if, with a given level of spending, a deficit of, say, $50 billion is financed by added taxation, it ceases by definition to be a deficit. But it does not follow that this is the best course to take. Whenever possible— except, say, in the midst of a major war—a deficit should be eliminated by reducing expenditures rather than by increasing taxes, because of the harm heavier taxes would probably do in discouraging and disorganizing production.

It is necessary to emphasize this point, because every so often some erstwhile advocate of big spending suddenly turns "responsible," and solemnly tells conservatives that if they want to be equally responsible it is now their duty to balance the budget by raising taxes to cover the existing and planned expenditures. Such advice completely begs the question. It tacitly assumes that the existing or planned level of expenditures, and all its constituent items, are absolutely necessary and must be fully covered by increased taxes no matter what the cost in economic disruption.

We have had thirty-nine deficits in the forty-seven fiscal years since 1931. The annual spending total has gone up from $3.6 billion in 1931 to $401.9 billion—112 times as much—in 1977. Yet the argument that we must keep on balancing this multiplied spending by equally multiplied taxation continues to be regularly put forward. The only real solution is to start slashing the spending before it destroys the economy.

Given a budget deficit, however, there are two ways in which it can be paid for. One is for the government to pay for its deficit outlays by printing and distributing more money. This may be done either directly or by the government's asking the Federal Reserve or the private commercial banks to buy its securities and to pay for them either by creating deposit credits or with newly issued inconvertible Federal Reserve notes. This of course is simple, naked inflation.

Or the deficit may be paid for by the government's selling its bonds to the public and having them paid for out of real savings. This is not directly inflationary, but it merely leads to an evil of a different kind. The government borrowing competes with and "crowds out" private capital investment, and so retards economic growth.

Let us examine this a little more closely. There is at any given time a total amount of actual or potential savings available for investment. Government statistics regularly give estimates of these. The gross national product in 1974, for example, was calculated to be $1,499 billion. Gross private saving for the same year was $215.2 billion—14.4 percent of GNP—of which $74 billion consisted of personal saving and $141.2 billion of gross business saving. But the federal budget deficit in that year was $11.7 billion, and in 1975 $73.4 billion, seriously cutting down the amount that could go into the capital investment necessary to increase productivity, real wages, and real long-run consumer welfare.

The government statistics estimate the amount of gross private domestic investment in 1974 at $215 billion and in 1975 at $183.7 billion. But it is probable that the greater part of this represented mere replacement of deteriorated, worn-out, or obsolete plant, equipment, and housing, and that net new capital formation was much smaller.

Let us turn to the amount of new capital supplied through the security markets. In 1973, total new issues of securities in the United States came to $99 billion. Of these, $32 billion consisted of private corporate stocks and bonds, $22.7 billion of state and local bonds and notes, $1.4 billion of bonds of foreign governments, and $42.9 billion of obligations of the U.S. government and its agencies. Thus of the combined total of $74.9 billion borrowed by the U.S. government and by private industry, the government got 57 percent and private industry only 43 percent.

Crowding Out

The crowding-out argument can be stated in a few elementary propositions: (1) Government borrowing competes with private borrowing. (2) Government borrowing finances government deficits. (3) What the government borrows is spent chiefly on consumption, but what private industry borrows chiefly finances capital investment. (4) It is the amount of new capital investment that is chiefly responsible for the improvement of economic conditions.

The possible total of borrowing is restricted by the amount of real savings available. Government borrowing crowds out private borrowing by driving up interest rates to levels at which private manufacturers who would otherwise have borrowed for capital investment are forced to drop out of the market.

Yet government spending and deficits keep on increasing year by year. Why? Chiefly because they serve the immediate interests of politicians seeking votes, but also because the public still for the most part accepts a set of sophistical rationalizations.

The whole so-called Keynesian doctrine may be summed up as the contention that deficit spending, financed by borrowing, creates employment, and that enough of it can guarantee "full" employment. The American people have even had foisted upon them the myth of a "full-employment budget." This is the contention that projected federal expenditures and revenues need not be, and ought not to be, those that would bring a real balance of the budget under actually existing conditions, but merely those that would balance the budget *if* there were "full employment."

To quote a more technical explanation (as it appears, for example, in the *Economic Report of the President,* January 1976): "Full employment surpluses or deficits are the differences between what receipts and expenditures are estimated to be if the economy were operating at the potential output level consistent with a 4 per cent unemployment" (p. 54).

A table in that report shows what the differences would have been for the years 1969 through 1975 between the actual budget and the so-called full-employment budget. For the calendar year 1975, for example, actual receipts were $283.5 billion and expenditures $356.9 billion, leaving an actual budget deficit of $73.4 billion. But in conditions of full employment, receipts from the same tax rate *might* have risen to $340.8 billion, and expenditures *might* have fallen to $348.3 billion, leaving a deficit not of $73.4 billion but only of $7.5 billion. Nothing to worry about.

Nothing to worry about, perhaps, in a dream world. But let us return to the world of reality. The implication of the full-employment budget philosophy (though it is seldom stated explicitly) is not only that in a time of high unemployment it would make conditions even worse to aim at a real balance of the budget, but that a full-employment budget can be counted on to *bring* full employment.

The proposition is preposterous. The argument for it assumes that the amount of employment or unemployment depends on the amount of added dollar "purchasing power" that the government decides to squirt into the economy. Actually the amount of unemployment is chiefly determined by entirely different factors, such as: the relations in various industries between selling prices and costs and between particular prices and particular wage-rates, the wage rates exacted by strong unions and strike threats, the level and duration of unemployment insurance and relief payments (making idleness more tolerable or attractive), and the existence and size of legal minimum-wage rates. But these and other important factors are persistently ignored by the full-employment budgeteers and by all the other advocates of deficit spending as the great panacea for unemployment.

It may be worthwhile, before we leave this subject, to point to one or two of the practical consequences of a consistent adherence to a full-employment budget policy. In the twenty-eight years from 1948 to 1975, there were only eight in which unemployment fell below the government target-level of 4 percent. In all the other years the full-employment budgeteers would have prescribed an actual deficit. But they say nothing about achieving a surplus in full-employment years, much less about its desirable size. Presumably they would consider any surplus at all, any repayment of the government debt, as extremely dangerous at any time. So a prescription for full-employment budgeting might not produce very different results in practice from a prescription for perpetual deficit. Perhaps an even worse consequence is that as long as this prescription prevails, it can only act to divert attention from the real causes of unemployment and their real cure.

Perhaps a word needs to be said about the fear of a surplus that has developed in recent decades—ever since about 1930, in fact. This of course is only the reverse side of the myth that a deficit is needed to "stimulate" the economy by "creating purchasing power." The only way in which a surplus could do even temporary harm would be by bringing about a sudden substantial reduction in the money supply. It could do this only if the bonds paid off were those held by the banking system against which demand deposits had been created. But in 1977, out of a gross public debt of $697.4 billion, $100.5 billion was held by commercial banks and $94.6 billion by Federal Reserve banks. This left $502.3 billion, or about 72 percent, in nonbanking hands. This could be retired, say, over fifty years, without shrinking the money supply in the least. And if the public debt were retired at a rate of $5 billion or $10 billion a year, private holders would have that much more to invest in private industry.

A myth even more pernicious than the full-employment budget, and akin to it in nature, is the Phillips curve. This is the doctrine that there is a "trade-off" between employment and inflation, and that this can be plotted on a precise curve—that the less inflation, the more unemployment, and the more inflation, the less unemployment. But since this incredible doctrine is more directly related to the issuance of currency than to government spending and deficits, we shall examine it later.

In conclusion: Chronic excessive government spending and chronic huge deficits are twin evils. The deficits lead more directly to inflation, and therefore, in recent years they have tended to receive a disproportionate amount of criticism from economists and editorial writers. But the total spending is the greater evil because it is the chief political cause of the deficits. If the spending were more moderate, the taxes to pay for it would not have to be so oppressive, so damaging to incentive, so destructive of employment and production. So the persistence and size of deficits, though serious, is a derivative problem; the primary evil is the exorbitant spending, the leviathan Welfare State. If spending were brought within reasonable bounds, taxes to pay for it would not have to be so burdensome and demoralizing, and politicians could be counted on to keep the budget balanced.

10

What Spending and Deficits Do Not Do

In the preceding chapter we have examined some of the harm that deficits do. Let us here concentrate on what they do not do. They do not cure unemployment.

Let us turn to segments of the historical record, year by year.

Year	Deficit ($ in Millions)	Percentage of Unemployment
1931	$ 462	15.9
1932	2,735	23.6
1933	2,602	24.9
1934	3,630	21.7
1935	2,791	20.1
1936	4,425	16.9
1937	2,777	14.3
1938	1,177	19.0
1939	3,862	17.2
1940	3,095	14.6

Sources: *Budget of the United States, 1978*, p. 437. *Historical Supplement to Economic Indicators, 1967*, p. 35.

After 1930, we had cheap money, inflexible or rising wage rates, and heavy government deficits for the next ten years. We also had mass unemployment for the next ten years—until World War II finally bailed us out.

In the foregoing tabulation, the deficits are for the fiscal years ending on June 30; the unemployment is an average of the full calendar year. These deficits may not seem large in comparison with the sums to which we have recently become accustomed, but they were not trivial in their time. As the average annual deficit for the period was $2.8 billion, and the average expenditure $6.7 billion, the deficits averaged 42 percent of total expenditures. Translated into other terms, the $2.8 billion average deficit was 3.6 percent of the gross national product of the period. The same percentage of the gross national product of 1976 would be equivalent to a deficit of $60.9 billion.

Now let us look at the record from 1960 through 1976.

Year	Deficit ($ in Millions)	Percentage of Unemployment
1960	+ 269★	5.5
1961	3,406	6.7
1962	7,137	5.5
1963	4,751	5.7
1964	5,922	5.2
1965	1,596	4.5
1966	3,796	3.8
1967	8,702	3.8
1968	25,161	3.6
1969	+3,236★	3.5
1970	2,845	4.9
1971	23,033	5.9
1972	23,372	5.6
1973	14,849	4.9
1974	4,668	5.6
1975	45,108	8.5
1976	66,461	7.7

★ Surplus.

Sources: *Budget of the United States, 1978,* p. 437. *Economic Report of the President,* January 1977, p. 221.

There are so many factors operating at all times in a national economy, and so many conditions, in particular, helping to determine the overall rate of employment or unemployment, that a simple statistical comparison like the foregoing does not prove anything beyond dispute. But on their face the figures hardly tend to show that deficits, even massive ones, prevent or even reduce unemployment. On the contrary, the clear trend is that the higher the deficits in the foregoing table, the worse the unemployment record.

The average unemployment in this country over a long period of years has been a shade under 5 percent. In the six years beginning 1971, when massive chronic deficits set in, the unemployment rate averaged 6.36 percent, and higher in the two years when the deficits were highest.

It is interesting that in the sixteen years following 1960, there was a surplus in only one year—1969—and in that year unemployment was the lowest shown in the table.

A coincidence, no doubt. But again, one of the worst consequences of the fixed Keynesian myth that deficit spending cures unemployment is not only that it promotes reckless government spending and monetary inflation, but that it systematically deflects attention from a study of the real causes of unemployment—excessive union wage rates, minimum wage laws, prolonged unemployment insurance, and a score of other social programs that diminish the incentives for men to accept market wages or to look for work.

11

Lessons of the German Inflation [1]

We learn from extreme cases, in economic life as in medicine. A moderate inflation, that has been going on for only a short time, may seem like a great boon. It appears to increase incomes and to stimulate trade and employment. Politicians find it profitable to advocate more of it—not under that name, of course, but under the name of "expansionary" or "full-employment" policies. It is regarded as politically suicidal to suggest that it be brought to a halt. Politicians promise to "fight" inflation; but by that they almost never mean slashing government expenditures, balancing the budget, and halting the money-printing presses. They mean denouncing the big corporations and other sellers for raising their prices. They mean imposing price and rent controls.

When the inflation is sufficiently severe and prolonged, however, when it becomes what is called a hyperinflation, people begin at

---

[1] For most of the statistics and some of the other information in this chapter I am indebted to two books: chiefly to Costantino Bresciani-Turroni, *The Economics of Inflation* (London: George Allen & Unwin, 1937), and partly to Frank D. Graham, *Exchange, Prices, and Production in Hyper-Inflation: Germany, 1920–1923* (Princeton: Princeton University Press, 1930; and New York: Russell & Russell, 1967). These authors in turn derived most of their statistics from official sources.

last to recognize it as the catastrophe it really is. There have been scores of hyperinflations in history—in ancient Rome under Diocletian, in the American colonies under the Continental Congress in 1781, in France from 1790 to 1796, in Austria, Hungary, Poland, and Russia after World War I, and in three or four Latin American countries today.

But the most spectacular hyperinflation in history, and also the one for which we have the most adequate statistics, occurred in Germany in the years from 1919 to the end of 1923. That episode repays the most careful study for the light it throws on what happens when an inflation is allowed to run its full course. Like every individual inflation, it had causes or features peculiar to itself—the Treaty of Versailles, with the very heavy reparation payments it laid upon Germany, the occupation of the Ruhr by Allied troops in early 1923, and other developments. But we can ignore these and concentrate on the features that the German hyperinflation shared with other hyperinflations.

At the outbreak of World War I—on July 31, 1914—the German Reichsbank took the first step by suspending the conversion of its notes into gold. Between July 24 and August 7 the bank increased its paper note issue by 2 billion marks. By November 15, 1923, the day the inflation was officially ended, it had issued the incredible sum of 92.8 quintillion (92,800,000,000,000,000,000) paper marks. A few days later (on November 20) a new currency, the rentenmark, was issued. The old marks were made convertible into it at a rate of one trillion to one.

It is instructive to follow in some detail how all this came about, and in what stages. By October 1918, the last full month of World War I, the quantity of paper marks had been increased fourfold over what it was in the prewar year 1913, yet prices in Germany had increased only 139 percent. Even by October 1919, when the paper money circulation had increased sevenfold over that of 1913, prices had not quite increased sixfold. But by January 1920 this relationship was reversed: money in circulation had increased 8.4 times and the wholesale price index 12.6 times. By November 1921 circulation had increased 18 times and wholesale prices 34 times. By November 1922 circulation had increased 127 times and wholesale prices 1,154 times, and by November 1923 circulation had increased 245 *billion* times and prices 1,380 *billion* times.

These figures discredit the crude or rigid quantity theory of money, according to which prices increase in proportion to the increase in the stock of money—whether the money consists of gold and convertible notes or merely of irredeemable paper.

And what happened in Germany is typical of what happens in every hyperinflation. In what we may call Stage One, prices do not increase nearly as much as the increase in the paper money circulation. This is because the man in the street is hardly aware that the money supply is being increased. He still has confidence in the money and in the preexisting price level. He may even postpone some intended purchases because prices seem to him abnormally high, and he still hopes that they will soon fall back to their old levels.

Then the inflation moves into what we may call Stage Two, when people become aware that the money stock has increased, and is still increasing. Prices then go up approximately as much as the quantity of money is increased. This is the result assumed by the rigid quantity theory of money. But Stage Two, in fact, may last only for a short time. People begin to assume that the government is going to keep increasing the issuance of paper money indefinitely, and even at an accelerating rate. They lose all trust in it. The result is Stage Three, when prices begin to increase far faster than the government increases, or even than it can increase, the stock of money.

(This result follows not because of any proportionate increase in the velocity of circulation of money, but simply because the value that people put upon the monetary unit falls faster than the issuance increases. See chapter 13 for a more detailed discussion of this point.)

Money versus Prices

But throughout the German inflation there was almost no predictable correspondence between the rate of issuance of new paper marks, the rise in internal prices, and the rise in the dollar-exchange rate. Suppose, for example, we assign an index number of 100 to currency circulation, internal prices, and the dollar rate in October 1918. By February 1920 circulation stood at 203.9, internal prices at 506.3, and the dollar rate at 1,503.2. One result was that prices of imported goods then reached an index number of 1,898.5.

But from February 1920 to May 1921 the relationship of these rates of change was reversed. On the basis of an index number of 100 for all of these quantities in February 1920, circulation in May 1921 had increased to 150.1, but internal prices had risen to only 104.6, and the dollar exchange rate had actually fallen to 62.8. The cost of imported goods had dropped to an index number of 37.5.

Between May 1921 and July 1922 the previous tendencies were once more resumed. On the basis of an index number of 100 for May 1921, the circulation in July 1922 was 248.6, internal prices were 734.6, and the dollar rate 792.2.

Again, between July 1922 and June 1923 these tendencies continued, though at enormously increased rates. With an index number of 100 for July 1922, circulation in June 1923 stood at 8,557, internal prices at 18,194, and the dollar rate at 22,301. The prices of imported goods had increased to 22,486.

The amazing divergence between these index numbers gives some idea of the disequilibrium and disorganization that the inflation caused in German economic life. There was a depression of real wages practically throughout the inflation, and a great diminution in the real prices of industrial shares.

How did the German hyperinflation get started? And why was it continued to this fantastic extent?

Its origin is hardly obscure. To pay for the tremendous expenditures called for by a total war, the German government, like others, found it far easier both economically and politically to print money than to raise adequate taxes. In the period from 1914 to October 1923, taxes covered only about 15 percent of expenditures. In the last ten days of October 1923, ordinary taxes were covering less than one percent of expenses.

What was the government's own rationalization for its policies? The thinking of the leaders had become incredibly corrupted. They inverted cause and effect. They even denied that there was any inflation. They blamed the depreciation of the mark on the adverse balance of payments. It was the rise of prices that had made it necessary to increase the money supply so that people would have enough money to pay for goods. One of their most respected monetary economists, Karl Helfferich, held to this rationalization to the end:

The increase of the circulation has not preceded the rise of prices and the depreciation of the exchange, but it followed slowly and at great distance. The circulation increased from May 1921 to the end of January 1923 by 23 times; it is not possible that this increase had caused the rise in the prices of imported goods and of the dollar, which in that period increased by 344 times.[2]

Of course such reasoning was eagerly embraced by Germany's politicians. In the late stages of the inflation, when prices rose far faster than new money could even be printed, the continuance and even acceleration of inflation seemed unavoidable. The violent rise of prices caused an intense demand for more money to pay the prices. The quantity of money was not sufficient for the volume of transactions. Panic seized manufacturers and business firms. They were not able to fulfill their contracts. The rise of prices kept racing ahead of the volume of money. The thirty paper mills of the government, plus its well-equipped printing plants, plus a hundred private printing presses, could not turn out the money fast enough. The situation was desperate. On October 25, 1923, the Reichsbank issued a statement that during the day it had been able to print only 120 *quadrillion* paper marks, but the demand for the day had been for a *quintillion!*

One reason for the despair that seized the Germans was their conviction that the inflation was caused principally by the reparations burden imposed by the Treaty of Versailles. This of course played a role, but far from the major one. The reparations payments did not account for more than a third of the total discrepancy between expenditure and income in the German budget in the whole four financial years 1920 through 1923.

In the early stages of the inflation German internal prices rose more than the mark fell in the foreign exchange market. But for the greater part of the inflation period—in fact, up to September 1923—the external value of the mark fell much below its internal value. This meant that foreign goods became enormously expensive for Germans while German goods became great bargains for foreigners. As a result, German exports were greatly stimulated, and so was activity and employment in many German industries. But this was later recognized as a false prosperity. Germany was in effect selling its production abroad much below real costs and

---

[2] Karl Helfferich, *Das Geld* (sixth edition, Leipzig, 1923).

paying extortionate prices for what it had to buy from abroad.

In the last months of the German inflation, beginning in the summer of 1923, internal prices spurted forward and reached the level of world prices, even allowing for the incredibly depreciated exchange. The exchange rate of the paper mark, calculated in gold marks, was 1,523,809 paper marks to one gold mark on August 28, 1923. It was 28,809,524 on September 25, 15,476,190,475 on October 30, and was "stabilized" finally at one trillion to one on November 20.

One change that brought about these astronomical figures is that merchants had finally decided to price their goods in gold. They fixed their prices in paper marks according to the exchange rate. Wages and salaries also began to be "indexed," based on the official cost-of-living figures. Methods were even devised for basing wages not only on the existing depreciation but on the probable future depreciation of the mark.

Finally, with the mark depreciating every hour, more and more Germans began to deal with each other in foreign currencies, principally dollars.

Experience That Did Not Educate

Viewed in retrospect, one of the most disheartening things about the inflation is that no matter how appalling its consequences became, they failed to educate the German monetary economists, or cause them to reexamine their previous sophisms. The very fact that the paper marks began to depreciate faster than they were printed (because everybody feared still further inflation) led these economists to argue that there was no monetary or credit inflation in Germany at all! They admitted that the stamped value of the paper money issued was enormous, but the "real" value—that is, the gold value according to the exchange rate—was far lower than the total money circulating in Germany before the war. This argument was expounded by Karl Helfferich in official testimony in June 1923. In the summer of 1922 Professor Julius Wolf wrote: "In proportion to the need, less money circulates in Germany now than before the war. This statement may cause surprise, but it is correct. The circulation is now 15–20 times that of pre-war days, while prices have risen 40–50 times." Another economist, Karl Elster, in his book on the German mark, declared: "However enor-

61

mous may be the apparent rise in the circulation in 1922, actually the figures show a decline"!

Of course all of the bureaucrats and politicians responsible for the inflation tried to put the blame for the soaring prices of everything from eggs to the dollar on to a special class of selfish and wicked people called "speculators"—forgetting that everybody who buys or sells and tries to anticipate future prices is unavoidably a speculator.

The Effect on Production

There is today still an almost universal belief that inflation stimulates trade, employment, and production. For the greater part of the German inflation, most businessmen believed this to be true. The depreciation of the mark stimulated their exports. In February and March 1922, when the dollar was rising, business seemed to reach a maximum of activity. The *Berliner Tageblatt* wrote in March of the Leipzig Fair: "It is no longer simply a zeal for acquiring, or even a rage: it is a madness." In the summer of 1922 unemployment practically disappeared. In 1920 and 1921, on the other hand, every improvement in the mark had been followed by an increase of unemployment.

The real effect of the inflation, however, was peculiarly complex. There were violent alternations of prosperity and depression, feverish activity and disorganization. Yet there were certain dominant tendencies. Inflation directed production, trade, and employment into channels different from those they had previously taken. Production was less efficient. This was partly the result of the inflation itself, and partly of the deterioration and destruction of German plant and equipment during the war. In 1922 (the year of greatest economic expansion after the war) total production seems to have reached no more than 70 to 80 percent of the level of 1913. There was a sharp decline in farm output.

High prices imposed "forced saving" on most of the German population (in the sense that they forced people to reduce the number of things they could consume). High paper-profit margins combined with tax considerations led German manufacturers to increase their investment in new plant and equipment. (Later much of this new investment proved to be almost worthless. As will be shown in chapter 16, this is an inevitable consequence of prolonged inflation.)

There was a great decline in labor efficiency. Part of this was the result of malnutrition brought about by high food prices. Bresciani-Turroni tells us: "In the acutest phase of the inflation Germany offered the grotesque, and at the same time tragic, spectacle of a people which, rather than produce food, clothes, shoes, and milk for its own babies, was exhausting its energies in the manufacture of machines or the building of factories."[3]

There was a great increase in unproductive work. As a result of changing prices and increased speculation, the number of middlemen increased continually. By 1923 the number of banks had multiplied fourfold over 1914. Speculation expanded pathologically. When prices were increasing a hundredfold, a thousandfold, a millionfold, far more people had to be employed to make calculations, and such calculations also took up far more time of old employees and of buyers. With prices racing ahead, the will to work declined. The production of coal in the Ruhr, which in 1913 had been 928 kilograms per miner, had decreased in 1922 to 585 kilograms. The "dollar rate" was the theme of all discussions.

Inefficient and unproductive firms were no longer eliminated. In 1913 there had been, on the average, 815 bankruptcies a month. They had decreased to 13 in August 1923, to 9 in September, to 15 in October, and to 8 in November. The acelerative depreciation of the paper mark kept wiping out everybody's real debt.

The continuous and violent oscillations in the value of money made it all but impossible for manufacturers and merchants to know what their prices and costs of production would be even a few months ahead. Production became a gamble. Instead of concentrating on improving their product or holding down costs, businessmen speculated in goods and the dollar.

Money savings (e.g., in savings bank deposits) practically ceased.

The novelist Thomas Mann has left us a description of the typical experience of a consumer in the late stages of the inflation:

> For instance, you might drop in at the tobacconist's for a cigar. Alarmed by the price, you'd rush to a competitor, find that his price was still higher, and race back

---

[3] *Economics of Inflation,* p. 197.

to the first shop, which may have doubled or tripled its price in the meantime. There was no help for it, you had to dig into your pocketbook and take out a huge bundle of millions, or even billions, depending on the date.[4]

But this doesn't mean that the shopkeepers were enjoying an economic paradise. On the contrary, in the final months of the inflation, business became demoralized. On the morning of November 1, 1923, for example, retail traders fixed their prices on the basis of a dollar exchange rate of 130 billion paper marks to one dollar. By afternoon the dollar rate had risen to 320 billion. The paper money that shopkeepers had received in the morning had lost 60 percent of its value!

In October and November, in fact, prices became so high that few could pay them. Sales almost stopped. The great shops were deserted. The farmers would not sell their products for a money of vanishing value. Unemployment soared. From a figure of 3.5 percent in July 1923, it rose to 9.9 percent in September, 19.1 percent in October, 23.4 percent in November and 28.2 percent in December. In addition, for these last four months more than 40 percent of union members were employed only part time.

The ability of politicians to profit from manufacturing more inflation had come to an end.

The Effect on Foreign Trade

Because the paper mark usually fell faster and further on the foreign exchange market than German internal prices rose, German goods became a bargain for foreigners, and German exports were stimulated. But the extent of their increase was greatly overestimated at the time. The relationship between the dollar rate and the internal price rise was undependable. When the mark improved on the foreign exchange market, exports fell off sharply. Germans in many trades viewed any improvement of the mark with alarm. The main long-run effect of the inflation was to bring about a continuous instability of both imports and exports. Moreover, the two were tied together. German industry largely worked with foreign raw materials; it had to import in order to export.

---

[4] Lecture, 1942; published in *Encounter,* 1975.

Germany did not "flood the world with its exports." It could not increase production fast enough. Its industrial output in 1921 and 1922, in spite of the appearance of feverish activity, was appreciably lower than in 1913. As I have noted before, because of price and foreign exchange distortions, Germany was in effect giving away part of its output.

But this loss had one notable offset. In the earlier stages of the inflation, foreigners could not resist the idea that the depreciated German mark was a tremendous bargain. They bought huge quantities. One German economist calculated that they probably lost seven-eighths of their money, or about 5 billion gold marks, "a sum triple that paid by Germany in foreign exchange on account of reparations."

The Effect on Securities

Those who have lived only in comparatively moderate inflations will find it hard to believe how poor a hedge the holding of shares in private companies provided in the German hyperinflation. The only meaningful way of measuring the fluctuation of German stock prices is as a percentage of changes in their gold (or dollar) value, or as a percentage of German wholesale prices. In terms of the latter, and on the basis of an index number of 100 for 1913, stocks were selling at an average of 35.8 in December 1918, 15.8 in December 1919, 19.1 in December 1920, 21 in December 1921, 6.1 in December 1922, and 21.3 in December 1923.

This lack of responsiveness is accounted for by several factors. Soaring costs in terms of paper marks forced companies continually to offer new shares to raise capital, with the result that what was being priced in the market was continually "diluted" shares. Mounting commodity prices, and speculation in more responsive hedges like the dollar, absorbed so large a proportion of the money supply that not much was left to invest in securities. Companies paid very low dividends. According to one compilation, 120 typical companies in 1922 paid out dividends equal, on the average, to only one-quarter of one percent of the prices of the shares.

The nominal profits of the companies were frequently high, but there seemed no point in holding them for distribution because they would lose so much of their purchasing power in the period between the time they were earned and the day the stockholder got them. They were therefore ploughed back into the business. But people desperately wanted a return, and they could make short-term loans at huge nominal rates of interest. (High interest rates also meant low capitalized values.)

Moreover, investors rightly suspected that there was something wrong with the nominal net profits that the companies were showing. Most firms were still making completely inadequate depreciation and replacement allowances or showing unreal profits on inventories. Many companies that thought they were distributing profits were actually distributing part of their capital and operating at a loss. Finally, over each company hung an "invisible mortgage" — its potential taxes to enable the government to meet the reparations burden. And over the whole market hung, in addition, the fear of Bolshevism.

Yet it must not be concluded that stocks were at all stages a poor hedge against inflation. True, the average of stock prices (in gold value on the basis of an index number of 100 for 1913) fell from 69.3 in October 1918 to 8.5 in February 1920. But most of those who bought at this level made not only immense paper profits but real profits for the next two years. By the autumn of 1921 speculation on the German Bourse reached feverish levels. "Today there is no one—," wrote one financial newspaper, "from lift-boy, typist, and small landlord to the wealthy lady in high society — who does not speculate in industrial securities."

But in 1922 the situation dramatically changed again. When the paper index is converted into gold (or into the exchange rate for the dollar) it fell in October of that year to only 2.72, the lowest level since 1914. The paper prices of a selected number of shares had increased 89 times over 1914, but wholesale prices had increased 945 times and the dollar 1,525 times.

After October 1922, once again, the price of shares rapidly began to catch up, and for the next year not only reflected changes in the dollar exchange rate, but greatly surpassed them. Given an index number in gold of 100 in 1913, the price of shares rose to 16.0 in July 1923, 22.6 in September, 28.5 in October, and 39.4 in November. When the inflation was over, in December 1923, it was 26.9. But this meant that shares ended up at only about one-fourth of their gold value in 1913.

The movement of share prices contributed heavily to the profound changes in the distribution of wealth brought about in the inflation years.

Interest Rates

In an inflation, lenders who wish to protect themselves against the probable further fall in the purchasing power of money by the time their principal is repaid, are forced to add a "price premium" to the normal interest rate. This elementary precaution was ignored for years by the German Reichsbank. From the early days of the war until June 1922 its official discount rate remained unchanged at 5 percent. It was raised to 6 percent in July, to 7 percent in August, 8 percent in September, 10 percent in November, 12 percent in January 1923, 18 percent in April, 30 percent in August, and 90 percent in September.

But even the highest of these rates did nothing to deter borrowing by debtors who expected to pay off in enormously depreciated marks. The result was that the Reichbank's policy kindled an enormous credit inflation, based on commercial bills, on top of the enormous government inflation based on treasury bills. After September 1923, a bank or private individual had to pay at a rate of 900 percent per annum for a loan from the Reichsbank. But even this was no deterrent. At the beginning of November 1923 the market rate for "call money" rose as high as 30 percent per day — equivalent to more than 10,000 percent on an annual basis.

The Monetary Reform

There is not space here for an adequate summary of the redistribution of wealth, the profound social upheaval, and the moral chaos brought about by the German inflation. I must reserve them for separate treatment, and move on to discuss the monetary reform that ended the inflation.

On October 15, 1923, a decree was published establishing a new currency, the rentenmark, to be issued beginning November 15. On November 20 the value of the old paper mark was "stabilized" at the rate of 4,200 billion marks for a dollar, or one trillion old paper marks for a rentenmark or gold mark. The inflation came to a sudden halt.

The result was called "the miracle of the rentenmark." Indeed, many economists find it difficult to this day to explain exactly why the rentenmark held its value. It was ostensibly a mortgage on the entire industrial and agricultural resources of the country. It was provided that 500 rentenmarks could be converted into a bond having a nominal value of 500 gold marks. But neither the rentenmarks nor the bond were actually made convertible into gold.

Moreover, the old paper marks continued to be issued at a fantastic rate. On November 16 their circulation amounted to 93 quintillion; it soared to 496 quintillion on December 31, and continued to rise through July of the following year.

Bresciani-Turroni is inclined to attribute the "miracle" of the rentenmark to the desperate need for cash (more and more people had stopped accepting paper marks), and to the word *wertbeständig* ("constant value") printed on the new money. The public, he thinks, "allowed itself to be hypnotized" by that word.

There is a more convincing explanation. Though paper marks continued to be issued against *commercial* bills, from November 16 on, the discounting of *treasury* bills by the Reichsbank was stopped. This meant that at least no more paper money was being issued on behalf of the government to finance its deficits. In addition, the Reichsbank intervened in the foreign exchange market. In effect it pegged the rentenmark at 4.2 to the dollar and the old marks at 4.2 trillion to the dollar. Germany was now on a dollar exchange standard!

The Stabilization Crisis

The effect was dramatic. In the last months of the inflation the German economy was demoralized. Trade was coming to a standstill, many people were starving in the towns, factories closed. As we have seen, unemployment in the trade unions, which had been 6.3 percent in August, rose to 9.9 percent in September, 19.1 percent in October, 23.4 percent in November, and 28.2 percent in December. (The inflation technically came to an end in mid-November, but its disorganizing effects did not.) But after that confidence quickly revived, and trade, production, and employment with it.

Bresciani-Turroni and other writers refer to the "stabilization crisis" that follows an inflation which has been brought to a halt. But after a hyperinflation has passed beyond a certain point, any so-called stabilization crisis is comparatively mild. This is because the inflation itself has brought so much economic disorganization.

When it is said that unemployment rose after the mark stabilization, the statement is true at best only as applied to a few months. Bresciani-Turroni's month-by-month tables of unemployment end in December 1923. Here is what happened in the nine months from October 1923 through June 1924:[5]

Month	Total Unemployed
October 1923	534,360
November 1923	954,664
December 1923	1,473,688
January 1924	1,533,495
February 1924	1,439,780
March 1924	1,167,785
April 1924	694,559
May 1924	571,783
June 1924	401,958

Thus by June 1924 unemployment had returned to the prestabilization figure.

There was a real stabilization crisis, but it showed itself in a different way. One of the things that happens in an inflation, and especially in a hyperinflation, is that labor is employed in different directions than the normal ones, and when the inflation is over, this abnormal demand disappears. During an inflation labor is drawn into luxury lines — furs, perfumes, jewelry, expensive hotels, nightclubs — and many essentials are comparatively neglected. In Germany labor went particularly into fixed capital, into the erection of new plant, and into the overexpansion of industries making "instrumental" goods. And then, suddenly, as one industrialist bluntly put it, many of these factories were found to be "nothing but *rubbish*." In many cases it was soon found to be a mistake even to keep them closed down in the hope of reopening later. The mere cost of maintenance was excessive. It was cheaper to demolish them.

---

[5] The figures do not include part-time workers or employees in public emergency projects, but only unemployed workers eligible for unemployment compensation. I am indebted to Prof. Günther Schmölders for supplying them.

In brief, when the inflation ended, the distortions and illusions to which it had given rise came to an end with it. Parts of the economy had been overdeveloped at the expense of the rest. The inflation had produced a great lowering of real wages. In the first months of 1924 a big increase took place in the average incomes of individual workers as well as in employment. The index of real incomes rose from 68.1 in January 1924 to 124 in June 1928. This led to a great increase in the demand for consumption goods, and to a corresponding fall in the production of capital or instrumental goods. There was suddenly recognized to have been a great over-production of coal, iron, and steel. Unemployment set in in these industries. But once more careful attention was paid to production costs, and there was a return to labor efficiency.

There was apparently a great shortage of working capital, if we judge by interest rates. In April and May 1924 the rate for monthly loans rose in Berlin to a level equivalent to 72 percent a year. But a large part of this reflected continuing distrust of the stability of the new currency. At the same time loans in foreign currencies were only 16 percent. And in October 1924, for example, when rates for loans in marks had fallen to 13 percent, loans in foreign currencies were down to 7.2 percent.

It would be difficult to sum up the whole German inflation episode better than Bresciani-Turroni himself did in the concluding paragraph of his great book on the subject:

> At first inflation stimulated production because of the divergence between the internal and external values of the mark, but later it exercised an increasingly disadvantageous influence, disorganizing and limiting production. It annihilated thrift; it made reform of the national budget impossible for years; it obstructed the solution of the Reparations question; it destroyed incalculable moral and intellectual values. It provoked a serious revolution in social classes, a few people accumulating wealth and forming a class of usurpers of national property, whilst millions of individuals were thrown into poverty. It was a distressing preoccupation and constant torment of innumerable families; it poisoned the German people by spreading among all classes the spirit of speculation and by diverting them from

proper and regular work, and it was the cause of incessant political and moral disturbance. It is indeed easy enough to understand why the record of the sad years 1919–23 always weighs like a nightmare on the German people.

These lines were first published in 1931. There is only one thing to add. The demoralization that the debasement of the currency left in its wake played a major role in bringing the Nazis and Adolf Hitler into power in 1933.

12

Where the Monetarists Go Wrong

In the last decade or two there has grown up in this country, principally under the leadership of Professor Milton Friedman, a school known as the Monetarists. The leaders sometimes sum up their doctrine in the phrase "Money matters," and even sometimes in the phrase "Money matters most."

They believe, broadly speaking, that the "level" of prices of commodities and services tends to vary directly and proportionately with the outstanding quantity of money and credit—that if the quantity of money (comprehensively defined) is increased 10 percent, the prices of commodities will increase 10 percent; that if the quantity of money is doubled, prices will double, and so on. (This, of course, is on the assumption that the quantity of goods remains unchanged. If this is increased also, the rise in prices due to a greater supply of money will be correspondingly less.)

This is called the quantity theory of money. It is not new, but very old. It has been traced by some economic historians to as far back as the French economist Jean Bodin in 1566, and by others to the Italian Davanzati in 1588. In its modern form it was most elaborately presented by the American Irving Fisher in *The Purchasing Power of Money* (1911) and in later books.

The Monetarists have added some refinements to this theory,

but principally they have devoted themselves to giving it detailed statistical support and drawing much different conclusions than did Fisher himself regarding an appropriate monetary policy.

When Fisher began writing, the gold standard was still dominant in practice. He proposed to keep it, but with a radical modification. He would have varied its gold content according to the variations of an official price index, so that the dollar should represent, instead of a constant quantity of gold, a constant quantity of purchasing power. Milton Friedman rejects the gold standard altogether. He would substitute for it a law prescribing the issuance of irredeemable paper money:

> My choice at the moment would be a legislated rule instructing the monetary authority to achieve a specified rate of growth in the stock of money. For this purpose, I would define the stock of money as including currency outside commercial banks plus all deposits of commercial banks. I would specify that the Reserve System shall see to it that the total stock of money so defined rises month by month, and indeed, so far as possible, day by day, at an annual rate of X percent, where X is some number between 3 and 5. The precise definition of money adopted, or the precise rate of growth chosen, makes far less difference than the definite choice of a particular definition and a particular rate of growth.[1]

It is with considerable reluctance that I criticize the Monetarists, because, though I consider their proposed monetary policy unfeasible, they are after all much more nearly right in their assumptions and prescriptions than the majority of present academic economists. The simplistic form of the quantity theory of money that they hold is not tenable; but they are overwhelmingly right in insisting on how much "money matters," and they are right in insisting that in most circumstances, and over the long run, it is the quantity of money that is most influential in determining the purchasing power of the monetary unit. Other things being equal, the more dollars that are issued, the smaller becomes the value of

---

[1] Milton Friedman, *Capitalism and Freedom* (Chicago: University of Chicago Press, 1962), p. 54.

each individual dollar. So at the moment the Monetarists are more effective opponents of further inflation than the great bulk of politicians and even putative economists who still fail to recognize this basic truth.

The Quantity Theory

What might be called the strict, or mechanical, quantity theory of money rests on greatly oversimplified assumptions. As formulated by Davanzati in 1588, the total existing stock of money must always buy the total existing stock of goods—no more, no less. So if the stock of money is doubled, and the supply of goods remains the same, the average level of prices must be doubled. Each monetary unit must then buy only half as much as before. As formulated by its modern exponents, the assumptions underlying the strict quantity theory of money are not much advanced from this. As "money is only wanted to buy goods and services," they argue, this proportional relationship must hold.

But this is not what happens. The truth in the quantity theory is that changes in the quantity of money are a very important factor in determining the exchange value of a given unit of money. This is merely to say that what is true of other goods is true of money also. The market value of money, like the market value of goods in general, is determined by supply and demand. But it is determined at all times by *subjective* valuations, and not by purely objective, quantitative, or mechanical relationships.

As we saw in our consideration of the German inflation of 1919–23, in a typical inflation we may roughly distinguish three stages. In the first stage prices do not rise nearly as fast as the quantity of money is being increased. For one thing, if there has been some slack in the economy, purchases made with the new money may mainly stimulate increased production. (This is the point so emphasized and overemphasized by Keynes. It can happen, however, only at the beginning of an inflation, and only under special circumstances.)

Apart from this possible early stimulative effect of an inflation, most people at first do not realize that an inflation of the currency has taken place. Some prices have risen, but many people, comparing them with the prices to which they have become accustomed, assume that these new prices are too high, and will soon fall back to "normal." They hold off buying, and increase their cash holdings. As a result, prices do not at first rise as much as the quantity of money has been increased.

If the inflation is slow and has occasional stops, prices tend to catch up with the rate of increase in the money supply, and for a while there may be a result much like what the strict quantity theory of money would predict, in which prices tend to rise roughly in proportion to the increase in the money stock.

But if the inflation (meaning the increase in the quantity of money) continues, and particularly if it accelerates, people begin to fear that it is a deliberate governmental policy, that it will go on indefinitely, and that prices will continue to soar. So they hasten to spend their money while it still has some value—that is, before prices rise still further. The result is that prices begin to rise far faster than the quantity of money has been increased, and finally far faster than it even can be increased.

So we have the paradoxical result that, in a hyperinflation, when the government is grinding out new currency units at an astronomical rate, prices rise so fast that the existing quantity of money is not sufficient for the volume of transactions, and we have mounting complaints of a "scarcity" of money. In the late stages of the German inflation of 1923, for example, the entire stock of paper money, though with a stamped value billions of times higher, had a gold exchange-value of only one-ninth of what it had before the inflation started. Of course the paper mark finally became utterly valueless, as had the French assignats in 1796 and the American Continental currency in 1781.[2]

It is for this reason that any inflation must finally end. But the point I am stressing here is that the strict quantity theory of money is not true (though it may appear to be true under certain circumstances and for limited periods). So far as quantity is concerned, it is the *expected future* quantity of money, rather than the immediately existing quantity, that determines the exchange value of the monetary unit.

---

[2] On the French assignats, see Andrew Dickson White, *Fiat Money Inflation in France* (Irvington-on-Hudson, New York: Foundation for Economic Education, 1959), p. 83 and *passim,* and on the German inflation of 1923, Costantino Bresciani-Turroni, *The Economics of Inflation* (London: George Allen & Unwin, 1937), pp. 80–81.

The Importance of Quality

The value of money, however, is determined not merely by its quantity—even its expected future quantity—but also by its quality. Currency issued by a shaky government, for example, will not have as much value, other things being equal, as currency issued by a strong "legitimate" government of long standing.

In recent years we have witnessed much more familiar illustrations of the effect of qualitative deterioration in the monetary unit. Scores of nations have repeatedly announced devaluations of their currency. Prices have begun to rise in those countries the very next day, before there has been any chance to increase the quantity of money any further.

Still more striking is what has happened when nations on a gold standard have announced their abandonment of it. The United States went off the gold standard in March 1933. By 1934, the average of wholesale prices had increased 14 percent over 1933, and by 1937, 31 percent. The U.S. formally abandoned gold convertibility again in August 1971. Wholesale prices had actually *fallen* by 2 percent from August of the year before; but by August of the year later they increased by 4.35 percent. With all gold discipline removed, wholesale prices rose more than 13 percent between 1972 and 1973, and more than 34 percent between 1972 and 1974.

One of the most striking illustrations of the importance of the *quality* of the currency occurred in the Philippines late in World War II. The forces under General Douglas MacArthur had effected a landing at Leyte in the last week of October 1944. From then on, they achieved an almost uninterrupted series of successes. Wild spending broke out in the capital city of Manila. In November and December 1944, prices in Manila rose to dizzy heights. Why? There was no increase in the money stock. But the inhabitants knew that as soon as the American forces were completely successful their Japanese-issued pesos would be worthless. So they hastened to get rid of them for whatever real goods they could get.[3]

What has helped to keep the strict mathematical quantity theory of money alive, in spite of experiences of the kind just cited, is the famous Irving Fisher equation: $MV = PT$. In this M stands for the

---

[3] I have never seen a reference to this striking event in any textbook on money. See the *New York Times*, January 30, 1945.

quantity of money, V for its velocity of circulation, P for the average price level of goods and services, and T for the volume of trade, or the quantity of goods and services against which money is exchanged.

So when the quantity of money remains unchanged, for example, and prices start to soar (or any similar discrepancy occurs) the quantity theorists are not at all disconcerted. They are provided in advance with an easy alibi: the velocity of circulation of money must have changed enough to account for the apparent discrepancy. True, this requires them sometimes to assume some remarkable things. I pointed out in the last chapter that in the late stage of the German inflation of 1919–23 the entire stock of paper money had a gold value only one-ninth that of the far smaller nominal money stock before the inflation began. This would require us to assume that the average velocity of circulation had increased in the meanwhile nine times.

The Fallacies of "Velocity"

This is not possible. The concept of the velocity of circulation of money as held by the quantity theorists and embodied in the Fisherine equation $MV = PT$, is quite fallacious. Strictly speaking, money does not "circulate"; it is exchanged against goods. When the turnover of money increases, the turnover of goods increases correspondingly.

(We have here an illustration of how the use of mathematical symbols may mislead an economist even in an elementary application. If $MV = PT$, and you double V, then it seems to follow that $2MV = 2PT$, and that this can be read as meaning that doubling V can double P. But if we spell out the equation as $M \times V = P \times T$, it can be seen that $M \times 2V$ does *not* necessarily equal $2P \times T$, but more likely $P \times 2T$. In fact, the equation $MV = PT$ does not mean what Irving Fisher and his disciples thought it meant. They considered MV the "money side" of the equation and PT the "goods side." But as Benjamin M. Anderson, Jr., long ago pointed out in a shrewd analysis, "Both sides of the equation are money sides. . . . The equation asserts merely that what is *paid* is equal to what is *received*."[4])

---

[4] Benjamin M. Anderson, Jr., *The Value of Money* (New York: Richard R. Smith, 1917, 1936), p. 161.

There are no reliable statistics on the velocity of circulation of hand-to-hand currency.[5] But we do have figures on the annual rate of turnover of demand bank deposits. As bank deposits in the United States cover about eight-ninths of the media of payment, these figures are an important index.

What is most striking, when we examine these figures, is first of all the wide discrepancy that we find between the rate of turnover of demand deposits in the big cities, especially New York, and the rate that we find in 226 other reporting centers. In December 1975 the average annual rate of turnover of demand deposits in these 226 small centers was 71.8. In six large cities outside of New York it was 118.7. When we come to New York City itself, the rate was 351.8. This does not mean that people in New York were furiously spending their money at nearly five times the rate of people in the small centers. (We must always remember that each individual can spend his dollar income only *once*.) The difference is accounted for mainly by two factors. The big corporations have their headquarters or keep their banking accounts in the big cities, and these accounts are much more active than those of individuals. And New York City especially, with its stock exchanges and commodity exchanges, is the great center of *speculation* in the United States.

Though the velocity of circulation of money (mainly in the form of bank deposits) increases with speculation, speculation itself does not indefinitely increase. In order for speculation to increase, willingness to part with commodities must increase just as fast as eagerness to buy them. It is rapidly *changing* ideas of commodity values—not only differences of opinion between buyer and seller, but changing opinions on the part of individual speculators—that are necessary to increase the volume of speculation.

The value of a commodity, a stock, or a house does not change in any predictable relationship to the number of times it changes

---

[5] Milton Friedman and Anna Jacobson Schwartz, in their *Monetary History of the United States: 1867–1960* (Princeton: Princeton University Press, 1963), do offer annual estimates and tables of "velocity of money" based on worksheets of Simon Kuznets made for another study. But they define this velocity as "the ratio of money income to the stock of money." This hardly makes it a *transactions* velocity. Moreover, they appear to attach very little commodity-price-determining importance to it: "Velocity is a relatively stable magnitude that has declined secularly as real income has risen" (p. 34).

hands. Nor does the value of a dollar. When 100 shares of a stock are sold, their value is not thereby necessarily depressed, because the shares are also bought. Every sale implies a purchase, and every purchase a sale. When a man buys a commodity, he "sells" money; but the seller of the commodity "buys" money. There is no necessary connection whatever between changes in the velocity of circulation of money and changes in the "level" of commodity prices. Velocity of money is merely a *resultant* of a complex of other factors, and not itself a *cause* of any important change whatever.[6]

Still another fallacy into which many quantity theorists (and not they alone) are apt to fall is the concept of a price "level." This is the partly unconscious assumption that when prices rise during an inflation they rise *uniformly*, so that when the official consumer price index has risen over a given period by, say, 10 percent, all prices in that period have risen just about 10 percent. This assumption is never made explicitly, otherwise it would be much easier to correct. But it is latent in the discussions of most journalists and politicians. It therefore leads them greatly to underestimate the harm done by inflation. For the greater part of that harm is precisely that different people's prices, wage rates, and incomes go up so unevenly and at different rates. This not only means great windfalls for some and tragedies for others, but it distorts and disrupts economic relationships. It unbalances, reduces, and misdirects production. It leads to unemployment and to malemployment. And attempts to correct this through such schemes as "indexing" only tend to increase the harm by magnifying the distortions.

I do not mean to suggest that all those who call themselves Monetarists make this unconscious assumption that an inflation involves this uniform rise of prices. But we may distinguish two schools of Monetarists. The first would prescribe a monthly or annual increase in the stock of money just sufficient, in their judgment, to keep prices stable. The second school (which the first might dismiss as mere inflationists) wants a continuous increase in the stock of money sufficient to raise prices steadily by a "small" amount—2 or 3 percent a year.

---

[6] I have treated this subject at greater length in an essay, "Velocity of Circulation," in *Money, the Market and the State: Economic Essays in Honor of James Muir Waller*, N. A. Beadles and L. A. Drewry, eds. (Athens, Ga.: University of Georgia Press, 1968).

Can Inflation "Creep"?

The late Professor Sumner H. Slichter of Harvard was the most prominent of these advocates of "creeping" inflation. He thought that a planned price rise of 2 or 3 percent a year would be about right. He forgot that even if the government could hold an inflationary price rise to a rate of only 2 percent a year it would mean an erosion of the purchasing power of the dollar by about one-half in each generation.

And it would not produce the results that Slichter expected of it. For inflation is always a swindle. It cannot be candidly and openly planned. People everywhere will take compensatory actions. If a price rise of 2 percent a year is announced as the official goal, lenders will immediately add 2 percent to the interest rate they would otherwise have asked, union leaders will add 2 percent to the wage increase they would otherwise have demanded, and so around the circle. Not only will the "creeping" inflation begin to race, but its effect on production and employment will be disruptive rather than stimulative.

But our concern here is not with the advocates of creeping inflation (in the sense of creeping price rises, at no matter how low an annual rate) but with the Monetarists strictly so called, that is, with those who recommend instructing government monetary authorities to increase the monetary stock every year only enough to keep prices from falling. What increase do the Monetarists think sufficient to accomplish their purpose?

Let us return to the prescriptions of the acknowledged leader of the school, Milton Friedman. We have seen that, in 1962, in his *Capitalism and Freedom,* he recommended that the Federal Reserve authorities be instructed to increase the total stock of money (including "all deposits of commercial banks") at an annual rate of somewhere between 3 and 5 percent. But three years later, in a memorandum prepared for a consultant's meeting with the Board of Governors of the Federal Reserve Board on October 7, 1965, we find him recommending "as the new target a rate close to the top of the desirable range of 4 to 6 per cent for M-2" (currency plus demand and time deposits).[7]

---

[7] Reprinted in *Dollars and Deficits,* Milton Friedman, ed. (Englewood Cliffs, N. J.: Prentice-Hall, 1968), p. 152.

Still later, in 1969, we find him scaling down this rate considerably, though with misgivings and vacillations: "A policy fairly close to the optimum would probably be to hold the absolute quantity of money constant. . . . However, this policy, too, seems to me too drastic to be desirable in the near future although it might very well serve as a long-term objective."

He then discusses the relative advantages of a one percent and of a 2 percent rate, and then goes on:

> I do not want to gloss over the real contradiction between these two policies, between what for simplicity I shall call the 5 per cent and the 2 per cent rules. There are two reasons for this contradiction. One is that the 5 per cent rule was constructed with an eye primarily to short-run considerations, whereas the 2 per cent rule puts more emphasis on long-run considerations. The more basic reason is that I had not worked out in full the analysis presented in this paper when I came out for the 5 per cent rule. I simply took it for granted, in line with a long tradition and a near-consensus in the profession, that a stable level of prices of final products was a desirable policy objective. Had I been fully aware then of the analysis of this paper, I suspect that I would have come out for the 2 per cent rule. . . .
>
> Either a 5 per cent rule or a 2 per cent rule would be far superior to the monetary policy we have actually followed. The gain from shifting to the 5 per cent rule would, I believe, dwarf the further gain from going to the 2 per cent rule, even though that gain may well be substantial enough to be worth pursuing. Hence I shall continue to support the 5 per cent rule as an intermediate objective greatly superior to the present practice.[8]

One hardly knows whether to twit Professor Friedman for tergiversation or praise him for remarkable candor. But his vacillations, as I hope to show, really point to the inherent difficulties in the Monetarists' proposals.

---

[8] Milton Friedman, *The Optimum Quantity of Money* (Chicago: Aldine Publishing Co., 1969), pp. 46–48.

I made a distinction earlier between the Monetarists strictly so called and the "creeping inflationists." This distinction applies to the intent of their recommended policies rather than to the result. The *intent* of the Monetarists is not to keep raising the price level but simply to keep it from falling, that is, simply to keep it "stable." But it is impossible to know in advance precisely what uniform rate of money-supply increase would in fact do this. The Monetarists are right in assuming that in a prospering economy, if the stock of money were not increased, there would probably be a mild long-run tendency for prices to decline. But they are wrong in assuming that this would necessarily threaten employment or production. For in a free and flexible economy prices would be falling because productivity was increasing, that is, because costs of production were falling. There would be no necessary reduction in real profit margins. The American economy has often been prosperous in the past over periods when prices were declining. Though money wage-rates may not increase in such periods, their purchasing power does increase. So there is no need to keep increasing the stock of money to prevent prices from declining. A fixed arbitrary annual increase in the money stock "to keep prices stable" could easily lead to a "creeping inflation" of prices.

This brings us to what I consider the fatal flaw in the Monetarist prescriptions. If the leader of the school cannot make up his own mind regarding what the most desirable rate of monetary increase should be, what does he expect to happen when the decision is put in the hands of the politicians?

We do not need to allow our fancies to roam very far. We already know the answer from what has been happening in the United States since we left the gold standard forty-five years ago, and from what has been happening, for that matter, in nearly every country in the world since the gold standard was abandoned. The decision regarding the national money-supply has already been in the hands of the politicians everywhere. And this situation has led practically everywhere to continuous and usually accelerating inflation.

Friedman would take the decision out of the discretion of appointed monetary authorities and make it a "legislative rule." But what rate would a popularly elected legislature set? We may be sure that it would pick a "safe" rate of monetary expansion—at least 6 percent a year to begin with—to make sure that there would be no depression or unemployment. But at the first feeble sign of unemployment or "recession," brought about by excessive union wage demands or any other of a score of factors, politicians seeking election or reelection would demand that the legislative monetary-increase rule be raised to 8 percent, 10 percent, or whatever rate the political scramble for office might suggest.

A Political Football

The prescribed rate would become a political football. The tendency nearly always would be for the highest bidder to win. For the belief in inflation as the master solution of every economic problem is not new in this generation. Throughout recorded history it has always been latent. Whenever there has been depression and unemployment it has always been popularly blamed on or identified with "not enough money." In 1776, in his *Wealth of Nations,* Adam Smith was pointing out that "no complaint is more common than that of a scarcity of money."

The fatal flaw in the Monetarist prescription, in brief, is that it postulates that money should consist of irredeemable paper notes and that the final power of determining how many of these are issued should be placed in the hands of government, that is, in the hands of the politicians in office. The assumption that these politicians could be trusted to act responsibly, particularly for any prolonged period, seems incredibly naive. The real problem today is the opposite of what the Monetarists suggest. It is how to get the arbitrary power over the stock of money *out* of the hands of government, *out* of the hands of politicians.

The solution to that problem cannot be offered in a few lines. I have postponed it to chapter 23, "The Search for an Ideal Money."

13

What Determines the Value of Money?

The Velocity of Money

We cannot fully understand the present American and world inflations, and the consequences to which they are likely to lead, unless we fully understand the causes that determine the purchasing power of money. Perhaps the greatest obstacle to this understanding today is the continued prevalence of an old but false theory.

The strict quantity theory of money and its "equation of exchange" have dominated and distorted the thinking of even some of the most respected monetary economists. A striking illustration is Bresciani-Turroni's discussion in his otherwise admirable history and analysis of the German hyperinflation of 1919–23, *The Economics of Inflation.*

Bresciani-Turroni treats the equation of exchange as an inescapable axiom. In his version it is not $MV = PT$, but "$MV = p1a + p2b + p3c$ . . . where M is the quantity of money issued, V the velocity of circulation, $a, b, c, \ldots$ the quantities of goods exchanged and $p1, p2, p3 \ldots$ the respective prices."

When he finds that in the late stages of the German inflation (and in the late stages of practically all other hyperinflations) prices of goods did not rise in proportion to the increase in the quantity of money but at a far faster rate, he assumes that this *must* have been—that it could *only* have been—because the velocity of circulation increased sufficiently to account for the discrepancy.

His method of arriving at the supposed increase in the velocity of circulation is as follows. He first assigns the presumed velocity of circulation of money in Germany in 1913 an arbitrary base rate of one. He then compares, for each year or month after the inflation began, the number of times the German money stock was increased with the number of times that wholesale or retail prices increased. He then divides the price increase by the money-stock increase, and assumes that the quotient must represent the increase in the velocity of circulation.

For example, at the end of 1922 the currency circulation of Germany was 213 times greater than in 1913. Wholesale prices were 1,475 times greater. The cost of living was 685 times greater. Therefore, he concludes, in 1922 the velocity of circulation in wholesale trade must have increased 6.92 times and in retail trade 3.21 times.

He applies the same formula to each year from 1914 through 1918, and then to every month of the five years from October 1918 to October 1923. His derived velocity rate begins to go up rapidly from August 1922. For the last month on his table, October 1923, he gives the velocity of money in retail trade as 10.43 times greater than in 1913 and in wholesale trade as 17.79 times greater.

These velocity figures, in my opinion, are absurd and impossible. There are several ways of showing why they must be.

Let us begin with the truism, so astonishingly overlooked, that each individual or family income can be spent only once. This means that in a society with a given economic organization and division of labor the *annual* velocity of circulation from year to year cannot change very much.

Bresciani-Turroni nowhere mentions this. He thinks he can explain the huge increases in velocity of circulation that he assumes took place from month to month. He refers, for example, to the fact that some salaried employees received their pay only once every three months. Suppose, then, he argues, that at the height of the inflation, instead of spending their quarterly pay checks over each quarter, these employees spent the entire amount in the first few days after the checks were received? Would not this explain the increased money velocity?

85

There are several things wrong with such an explanation. First, those who were paid quarterly in the Germany of the early 1920s must have been a very small portion of the population. Second, it would not be easy to buy three months' supplies of everything in the first day or two. A three-months' family food supply, for example, could not be stored at home or kept fresh there. And if most of these quarterly payments or attempted expenditures fell on the same day, merchants would simply not have the goods in stock to sell.

Third, even if this kind of speed-up happened, it would not lead to a quarterly increase in velocity of circulation or even to much of a monthly increase. If a man spends his whole ninety-days' income on the first day, he has nothing to spend on any of the next ninety days. The *average* quarterly rate of spending does not change. So if, at the height of the inflation, every family in Germany was paid daily, and spent the whole of each day's income on the day it was received, then it spent one-365th of it every day instead of one-52nd of it every week. The monthly rate did not change much.

But there is still another and much more fundamental reason why Bresciani-Turroni's velocity-of-money conclusions are unacceptable. The very phrase "velocity of circulation," as I pointed out in the last chapter, embodies a false concept. Money does not literally circulate. This is a metaphor. Money is exchanged for goods and services. It is hardly possible to spend money without, by the same action, buying goods. (The borrowing or repayment of money loans constitutes a relatively small part of the total transfer of money, and so long as it does not increase or decrease the outstanding money stock it does not necessarily have much effect on the exchange value of the money unit.) Therefore it is hardly possible to speed up the velocity of circulation of money without speeding up to an approximately equal extent the velocity of circulation of goods. And if one does this (as Bresciani-Turroni himself admits) the exchange value of the money unit is not thereby depressed.

But in fact the sale of goods cannot be increased for any prolonged period beyond a very limited amount. (By a "prolonged period" I refer to anything beyond a couple of months.) This is true for the simple reason that the volume of goods for sale just cannot be increased by much in a short time. Bresciani-Turroni's tables show the average velocity of circulation of money to have increased in the first nine months of 1923 to an average of 8.25 times that of 1913. But this would practically have to mean that the quantity of goods sold in those nine months—and therefore, in effect, the quantity of goods *produced* in those nine months—must have been 8.25 times as great as the quantity produced in the corresponding nine months of 1913.

This is not only incredible on its face; it is known to have been untrue in Germany in 1923. For by Bresciani-Turroni's own account, production was disorganized by the inflation in 1923, and fell substantially.

There is still another factor that the assumption of a hugely increased velocity of money in a hyperinflation overlooks. In order for such an increase to occur, it is not merely necessary that the holders of money should be eager to get rid of it as quickly as possible, but that the sellers of goods should be correspondingly ready to part with their goods for money. But Bresciani-Turroni himself tells us, "The risk of transactions effected by payment in paper marks became so great in the summer of 1923 that many producers and merchants preferred not to sell at all, rather than accept in exchange a money subject to rapid depreciation."[1]

It is instructive to notice that Bresciani-Turroni in the end distrusts his own figures and his own explanation. He carries his own calculations only up to October 1923, when, as we have seen, he estimates that the average velocity of circulation of money must have been some fourteen times as great as in 1913. But he tells us that "in August 1923 the value of the paper money in circulation amounted on some days to scarcely 80 million gold marks"[2] (compared with 6,000 million in 1913). But on his own basis of calculation, as presented in his annual and monthly tables, this would require us to assume that on these days velocity of circulation must have been seventy-five times as great as the 1913 rates. Moreover, he also tells us that "on November 15th [1923]—on the eve of the cessation of the discount of Treasury bills by the Reichsbank— based on the *official* value of the gold mark (six hundred billion paper marks), the total value of the notes of the Reichsbank in circulation was 154.7 million gold marks. But based on the ex-

---

[1] *Economics of Inflation*, p. 174.
[2] *Ibid*.

change rate of the paper mark in New York the total value was as low as 97.4 million gold marks."

So based on the offical value of the gold mark, Bresciani-Turroni would have had to conclude that the velocity of circulation must have increased about thirty-nine times over 1913, and based on the paper mark exchange rate in New York, sixty-two times over 1913.

He draws no such conclusion and cites neither figure. Instead, he completely shifts his explanation of the decline in value of the paper mark. He then decides that "the increase in the velocity of circulation . . . does not completely explain the very great reduction of the total real value of the paper money, . . . for the place of the paper mark was taken by foreign exchange" and the return of metallic money to circulation.[3]

The "Cash Balance" Approach

I should like to add here that I not only regard an increase in the velocity of circulation as a totally false explanation of a rise in prices more rapid than the rise in the quantity of outstanding money in a hyperinflation, but that I consider an alternative explanation adopted by a number of economists—the "cash holdings," or "cash balance," approach—as also quite inadequate, especially in certain formulations.

Some economists formulate the cash holdings approach as follows: At the beginning of an inflation, prices generally do not rise as fast as the quantity of money is increased, because people think that prices have risen to unsustainable levels and will soon fall back to "normal." They hold off many purchases and add to their cash holdings. This in itself keeps prices from rising as much as the quantity of money has been increased. But when people finally come to fear that the inflation is going to be prolonged, and that the rise of prices may go on indefinitely, they begin to buy in advance. They pull down their cash holdings. It is this action that increases the rate at which prices begin to rise.

There are two major defects in this explanation. One is that, even if otherwise correct, it would account only for a relatively

---

[3] *Ibid.*, pp. 173–74.

small change in prices compared with the rate of monetary increase. Suppose people normally kept as an average cash balance the equivalent of 10 percent of their annual incomes, or roughly enough to spend over the next thirty-six days. If, in an inflation, they were willing to let their cash balances fall even to zero, this would only add some 10 or 11 percent to the total "active" money use. It could not account for the almost incredible fall in the purchasing power of the monetary unit, when compared even with the increase in the money stock, that occurs in a hyperinflation.

The other major defect in the cash holdings approach is that, no matter how much or often individuals decide to spend, the *average* cash holdings of *all* individuals in the country *cannot* be reduced! If a country has a population of approximately 200 million, and the total money supply is $800 billion (counting currency in the hands of the public, plus both demand and time bank deposits), then the average cash holding of each individual must be $4,000. The money must always be held by *someone*. What Peter spends, Paul receives. If half the people in the country, by increasing their spending, reduce their cash holdings by an average of $1,000 each, the other half must increase their cash holdings by the same average amount.

Subjective Value

What, then, *is* the basic explanation for the value of money, and for changes in that value?

It is the same as the explanation for the value of anything else. It is the subjective valuation that each of us puts on it. The objective purchasing power, or exchange value, of the monetary unit is derived from the composite of these subjective valuations. It is not, however, merely a physical or arithmetical composite of these individual subjective valuations. Individual valuations are themselves greatly influenced by what each of us finds to be the market, or "social," value. Just as hydrogen and oxygen may combine to form a substance—water—that seems to bear little resemblance to either, so the social, or market, valuation of money as well as other things is akin to a sort of chemical rather than an arithmetical combination of individual valuations.

All valuation begins in the minds of individuals. We are accustomed to saying that market value is determined by supply and demand, and this is as true of money as of other commodities. But we should be careful not to interpret either *supply* or *demand* in purely physical terms, but rather in psychological terms. *Demand* rises when people want something more than they did before. It falls when they want it less. *Supply* is more often thought of in a purely physical sense, but as an economic term it also refers to psychic factors. It may vary with price. At a higher price producers may make more of a commodity, or be ready to offer more of the existing stock for sale.

When it comes to money, economists have been too prone to explain value in purely physical or mathematical terms. Hence the strange vogue of the rigid proportional quantity theory of money, of the algebraic "equation of exchange," and of the alleged determining role played by the velocity of circulation of money.

What is overlooked is that the equation of exchange is a mathematical delusion. It is not an equation, as imagined, with money on the left side and goods on the right. There is no meaningful way in which all goods and services can be added to each other except in terms of their money prices. There is no meaningful way, for example, in which a pound of gold watches, a dozen square yards of cotton, a ten-room house, and a ton of sand can be added together except in terms of their individual prices in *money*. What we are adding is the amount of money required to buy them. Therefore the product of the equation of exchange, on each side, is a *sum of money*. These sums are equal because they are *identical*. The equation merely asserts that what is *paid* is equal to what is *received*. Neither the quantity theory nor the equation of exchange contains any proof of causation.[4] And the number of times that a unit of money changes hands has no necessary connection with the "level" of prices.

What is called the cash balance approach is less fallacious than the mechanical quantity theory of money. It does contain an element of truth, but in some formulations it confuses cause and effect. It is true that when people think that the value of money is going to rise — in other words, when they think commodity prices are going to decline — they tend to spend less money immediately. And when they think the value of money is going to fall — that

---

[4] For an elaboration of this analysis, see Benjamin M. Anderson, Jr., *The Value of Money* (New York: Richard R. Smith, 1917, 1936), ch. 13.

is, that commodity prices are going to rise — they tend to spend more money immediately. But the cash balance approach puts too much emphasis on a physical act and too little on the subjective change of valuation that prompts the act. The value of money does not decline because people try to speed up their spending; they speed up their spending because they think the purchasing power of their money is going to decline.

We can understand this better if we consider the purchase and sale of shares on the stock exchange. Suppose during a day's session American Steel publishes an unexpectedly favorable quarterly earnings report, that 10,000 shares are traded in, and that the price rises from 30 to 40. The price has not risen because Jones, Smith, and Watson have bought 10,000 shares from Brown, Green, and Doakes. After all, as many shares have been sold as bought. The price rises because both buyers and sellers now estimate the value of American Steel shares higher than they did before. Suppose, again, that National Motors closed at 35 on Monday, that after the close the directors unexpectedly fail to declare the regular dividend, and that the stock opens Tuesday morning at 25. This sort of thing happens frequently. There have been meanwhile no sales on which to blame the decline. The stock has fallen in price simply because both buyers and sellers now put a lower estimate on it. This is precisely what happens with the value of money. It is changes in value estimates that count, not changes in cash balances.

And this is why, in the late stages of a hyperinflation, prices start to soar far faster than the supply of money is increased and even far faster than it can be increased. Nearly everybody is convinced that the inflation is going to go on, that the printing of paper money will be more and more accelerated, that prices will rise at a faster and faster rate. They want to exchange their money for anything they can get. Finally, however, holders of goods refuse to accept that money on any terms.

Thus every inflation must eventually be ended by government or it must "self-destruct" — but not until after it has done untold harm.

14

Inflation and Unemployment

For many years it has been popularly assumed that inflation increases employment. This belief has rested on both naive and sophisticated grounds.

The naive belief goes like this: When more money is printed, people have more "purchasing power"; they buy more goods, and employers take on more workers to make more goods.

The more sophisticated view was expounded by Irving Fisher in 1926:

> When the dollar is losing value, or in other words when the price level is rising, a businessman finds his receipts rising as fast, on the average, as this general rise of prices, but not his expenses, because his expenses consist, to a large extent, of things which are contractually fixed.... Employment is then stimulated—for a time at least.[1]

---

[1] Irving Fisher, "A Statistical Relation between Unemployment and Price Changes," *International Labor Review*, June 1926, pp. 785–92. Milton Friedman has recently called attention to this article.

This view contains a kernel of truth. But thirty-two years after it appeared, in 1958, the British economist A. W. Phillips published an article which seemed to show that over the preceding century, when money wage-rates rose, employment rose, and vice versa.[2]

This, too, seemed a plausible relationship. Given a period for the most part noninflationary, but in which capital investment and invention were raising the unit-productivity of labor, profit margins on employment would be rising, in some years much more than in others; and in these years the demand for labor would increase, and employers would bid up wage rates. The increased demand for labor would lead both to higher wages and to increased employment. Phillips may have seen what he thought he saw.

But Keynesian economists, struck by the Phillips thesis, and seeing in it a confirmation of their previous belief, carried it much further. They began to construct Phillips curves of their own, based not on a comparison of wage rates and employment, but of general prices and employment. And they announced that they had found there a trade-off between unemployment and prices. Price stability and reasonably full employment, they asserted, just cannot exist at the same time. The more we get of the one the less we can have of the other. We must make a choice. If we choose a low level of inflation, or none at all, we have to reconcile ourselves to a high level of unemployment. If we choose a low level of unemployment, we must reconcile ourselves to a high rate of inflation.

This alleged dilemma has served as a rationalization for continued inflation in many countries when every other excuse has run out.

The Myth of the Phillips Curve

The Phillips curve is a myth, and in the last few years it has been increasingly recognized as a myth. The accompanying table compares the percent changes in the consumer price index for the twenty-eight years from 1948 to 1975, inclusive, with the percent rate of unemployment in the same years.

---

[2] A. W. Phillips, "The Relation between Unemployment and the Rate of Change of Money Wage Rates in the United Kingdom, 1861–1957," *Economica*, November 1958, pp. 283–99.

Year	Percent Change CPI	Percent Unemployment
1948	7.8	3.8
1949	−1.0	5.9
1950	1.0	5.3
1951	7.9	3.3
1952	2.2	3.0
1953	0.8	2.9
1954	0.5	5.5
1955	−0.4	4.4
1956	1.5	4.1
1957	3.6	4.3
1958	2.7	6.8
1959	0.8	5.5
1960	1.6	5.5
1961	1.0	6.7
1962	1.1	5.5
1963	1.2	5.7
1964	1.3	5.2
1965	1.7	4.5
1966	2.9	3.8
1967	2.9	3.8
1968	4.2	3.6
1969	5.4	3.5
1970	5.9	4.9
1971	4.3	5.9
1972	3.3	5.6
1973	6.2	4.9
1974	11.0	5.6
1975	9.1	8.5

Source: *Economic Report of the President,* January 1976, pp. 199 and 224.

I leave it to the Phillipsians to make what they can of this table. The average annual price rise in the twenty-eight years was 3.2 percent, and the average unemployment rate 4.9 percent. If the alleged Phillips relationship held dependably, then in any year in which the price rise (or "inflation" rate) went above 3.2 percent, the unemployment rate would fall below 4.9 percent. Conversely, in any year in which the "inflation" rate fell below 3.2 percent, the unemployment rate would rise above 4.9 percent. This relationship would hold for all of the twenty-eight years. If, on the other hand, the Phillips curve were inoperative or nonexistent, the probabilities are that the relationship would hold only about half the time. This is exactly what we find. The Phillips relation occurred in fifteen of the twenty-eight years but was falsified in the other thirteen.

(The consumer price index rose 5.8 percent in 1976 and 6.5 percent in 1977. Unemployment was 7.7 percent in 1976 and 7.0 percent in 1977. So if we add the results of these two years to the figures in the table we find that the Phillips relation occurred in fifteen of the thirty years and was falsified in fifteen.)

More detailed analysis of the table hardly helps. An economist who saw what happened only in the years 1948 through 1964 might have been excused for being impressed by the Phillips curve, for its posited relationship held in thirteen of those seventeen years. But an economist who saw only what happened in the last eleven of those twenty-eight years—from 1965 through 1975—might have been equally excused for suspecting that the real relationship was the exact oppostite of what the Phillips curve assumed, for in that period it was borne out in only two years and falsified in nine. And even the economist who seriously studied only what happened in the 1948–64 period would have noted some strange anomalies. In 1951, when the CPI rose 7.9 percent, unemployment was 3.3 percent; in 1952, when prices rose only 2.2 percent, unemployment *fell* to 3.0; and in 1953, when prices rose only 0.8 percent, unemployment fell further to 2.9.

Phillips statisticians can play with these figures in various ways, to see whether they can extract any more convincing correlation. They can try, for example, to find whether the Phillips relationship holds any better if the CPI rise is measured from December to December, or if the calculations are remade to allow for a lag of three months, or six months, or a year, between the "inflation" rate and the unemployment rate. But I do not think they will have any better luck. If the reader will make the count allowing for one year's lag between the price rise and the unemployment figure, for example, he will find the Phillips curve contention borne out in only ten years and contradicted in the other eighteen.

(I have referred to the rate of the consumer-price rise as the "inflation" rate because that is unfortunately the way the term is applied by the majority of journalists and even economists. Strictly, the term *inflation* should refer only to an increase in the stock of money. A rise of prices is a usual consequence of that increase, though the price rise may be lower or higher than the money increase. Insistence on the distinction between these two terms is not merely pedantic. When the chief consequence of an inflation is itself called the inflation, the real relation of cause and effect is obscured or reversed.)

A clearer picture of the relationship (or nonrelationship) of price rises and unemployment emerges if we take only the last fifteen years of the twenty-eight and make our comparisons for the average of five-year periods:[3]

	CPI Rise Rate (per year)	Unemployment Rate (per year)
1961–65	1.3%	5.5%
1966–70	4.3	3.9
1971–75	6.8	6.1

In sum, the highest rate of "inflation" was accompanied by the highest rate of unemployment.

The experience in other nations has been even more striking. In August 1975 the Conference Board published a study comparing the percentages of work forces *employed* with consumer price indices in seven industrial nations over the preceding fifteen years. By this measurement, in the United States, Canada, and Sweden, the relationship did not noticeably belie the Phillips curve. (In our twenty-eight year U.S. table, however, we saw that when the price-increase figure shot up in 1974 to 11 percent from a rate of 6.2 percent in 1973, unemployment also rose. If we look at 1975—not shown in the Conference Board study—we find that unemployment soared to 8.5 percent even though there was a similar high price rise—9.1 percent—in 1975. Similarly, if we take what happened in 1975 in Canada, we find that though consumer prices rose in that year by the unusually high rate of 10.7 percent, the index of manufacturing employment in Canada *fell* from 108.9 in 1974 to 102.8 in 1975.)

---

[3] This table was suggested by one which appeared in Milton Friedman's *Newsweek* column of December 6, 1976. I have made some minor changes.

In the four other countries in the Conference Board study, the relationship of employment and inflation was emphatically the opposite of that assumed by the Phillips curve. The steady price rise in Germany from 1967 to 1973 was accompanied by an equally steady fall in employment. In Japan a rise of 19 percent in consumer prices in 1973 and of 21 percent in 1974 was accompanied by a fall in employment. In Italy, though consumer prices began to soar in 1968, reaching a 25 percent annual rate in 1974, employment declined during the period. In some ways the record of Great Britain, where the Phillips curve was invented, was the worst of all. Though consumer prices soared 18 percent in 1974 from a rate of 4 percent a decade earlier, employment turned downward. Not shown in the Conference Board compilation was the record of 1975 itself, when the British CPI soared 24 percent—and employment fell further.

But informed economists with memories did not need to wait for the experience of the seventies to distrust the relationship posited by the Phillips curve. In the last and worst months of the great German hyperinflation of 1919–23, unemployment in the trade unions, which had been 6.3 percent in August 1923, soared to 9.9 percent in September, 19.1 percent in October, 23.4 percent in November, and 28.2 percent in December.

How We Buy Unemployment

There is a whole nest of fallacies wrapped in the Phillips curve, and one of them is the implication that the absence of inflation is the sole or at least the chief cause of unemployment. There can be scores of causes for unemployment. One is tempted to say that there can be as many distinguishable causes for unemployment as there are unemployed. But even if we look only at the unemployment brought about by governmental policies, we can find at least a dozen different types of measures that achieve this—minimum-wage laws, laws granting special privileges and immunities to labor unions and imposing special compulsions on employers to make concessions (in the U.S., the Norris–La Guardia Act, Wagner-Taft-Hartley Act, etc.), unemployment insurance, direct relief, Social Security payments, food stamps, and so on. Whenever unions are given the power to enforce their demands by strike threats and intimidation or by compulsory "collective bargaining" legally imposed on employers, the unions almost invariably extort above-market wage rates that bring about unemployment. Unemployment insurance becomes increasingly generous year by year, and at the time of writing is paid in some states for as long as sixty-five weeks. A study prepared for the U.S. Department of Labor in February 1975 finally conceded that "the more liberal the unemployment insurance benefits, the higher the unemployment rate will be."

As long ago as 1934, when the New Deal was being enacted, economist Benjamin M. Anderson remarked to me in conversation, "We can have just as much unemployment as we want to pay for." The government is today buying a huge amount of it. Yet when the monthly unemployment figures are published, the overwhelming majority of commentators and politicians forget all about this and attribute the high unemployment figure to insufficient federal spending, insufficient deficits, insufficient inflation.

Another thing wrong with the Phillips curve is the blind trust its compilers place in the official unemployment statistics. I am not speaking here merely about the amount of guesswork and sampling errors embodied in such statistics, but about the vagueness in the very concept of "full employment." Full employment never means that everybody has a job, but merely that everybody in the "labor force" has a job. And an immense amount of guesswork goes into estimating the labor force. Out of a total population estimated in 1975 at 213,631,000, only 92,613,000—or some 43 percent—were estimated as being in the "civilian labor force." These were part of the "noninstitutional" population sixteen years of age and over, with certain deductions. As only 84,783,000 persons were estimated as being employed in 1975, this left an average of 7,830,000 "unemployed."

But none of these figures involved exact counts. They were all estimates subject to various degrees of error. In any case, the unemployed can never be exactly counted because of the subjective element. As the economist A. C. Pigou put it some forty-five years ago, "A man is only unemployed when he is *both* not employed and *also* desires to be employed."[4]

---

[4] A. C. Pigou, *The Theory of Unemployment* (London: Macmillan, 1933), p. 3.

It is this second requirement that we can never measure. The U.S. Bureau of Labor Statistics counts a man as unemployed if he is out of a job and "looking for work." But it is very difficult to determine whether a man is actually looking for a job or how much effort he is making. And when men and women are being paid enough unemployment insurance or relief or food stamps to feel no great urgency to take a job, the raw government statistics can give a very misleading impression of the hardships of all unemployment.

Full employment, as bureaucratically defined, is a completely unrealistic goal. It has never been realized in the official figures. Even if there were no governmental policies that created unemployment, it is hardly possible to imagine a situation in which, on the very day any person was laid off, he found a new job with wages and other conditions to his liking. People who give up jobs, and even those who are dropped from them, commonly give themselves an intentional vacation. There is always a certain amount of "frictional," "normal," or "natural" unemployment—averaging in this country, as officially measured, about 5 percent—and persistent government interventions to force the figure below this average tend to create inflation and other distortions much worse than the alleged evil they are intended to cure.

When we put aside all questions of exact quantitative determination and alleged Phillips curves, it is nonetheless clear that inflation does affect employment in numerous ways. It is true that, at its beginning, inflation can tend to create more employment, for the reason that Irving Fisher gave long ago: It tends to increase sales and selling prices faster than it increases costs. But this effect is only temporary and occurs only to the extent that the inflation is unexpected. For in a short time costs catch up with retail selling prices. To prevent this the inflation must be continued. But as soon as people *expect* the inflation to be continued, they all make compensating adjustments and demands. Unions ask for higher wage rates and "escalation" clauses, lenders demand higher interest rates, including "price premiums," and so on. To keep stimulating employment, it is not enough for the government to continue inflating at the old rate, however high; it must accelerate the inflation. But as soon as people *expect even the acceleration*, this too becomes futile for providing more employment.

To set up "full employment at whatever cost" as the sole or

even chief economic goal, results in a distortion and perversion of all values.[5]

Meanwhile, even if the inflation is relatively mild and proceeds at a fairly even rate, it begins to create distortions in the economy. It is amazing how systematically this is overlooked. Most journalists and even most economists make the tacit assumption that an inflation increases prices *uniformly*—that if the wholesale or consumer price index has gone up about 10 percent in the last year, *all* prices have gone up about 10 percent. This assumption is seldom made consciously and *explicitly*; if it were it would be more often detected and refuted, for it is never correct. Even apart from the wide differences in the elasticity of demand for different commodities, the new money that the government prints and pays out in an inflation does not go proportionately or simultaneously to everybody. It goes, say, to government contractors and their employees, and these first receivers spend it on the particular goods and services they want. The producers of these goods, and their employees, in turn spend the money for still other goods and services. And so on. The first groups spend the money when prices have gone up least, the final groups when prices have gone up most. In addition, the growing realization that inflation will continue itself changes the direction of demand—away from thrift and toward luxury spending, for example.

Employment Misdirected

Thus while inflation is going on it always brings about a misdirection of production and employment. It leads to a condition of temporary demand for various products, a malproduction and a malemployment, a misallocation of resources, that neither can nor should be continued once the inflation is brought to a halt. Thus at the end of every inflation there is certain to be what is called a "stabilization crisis."

But even the distorted and misdirected employment cannot be indefinitely maintained by continuing or accelerating the inflation. For the inflation, as it goes on, more and more distorts *relative*

---

[5] The present writer has discussed this question more fully in ch. 26, "'Full Employment' as the Goal," *The Failure of the "New Economics"* (New Rochelle, N.Y.: Arlington House, 1959).

prices and *relative* wages, and disrupts workable relations between particular prices and particular wage rates. While some producers confront swollen and unmeetable demand, others are being driven out of business by wages and other costs rising far faster than their own selling prices. And as inflation accelerates it becomes impossible for individual producers to make any dependable estimate of the wage rates and other costs they will have to meet in the next few months, or their own future selling prices, or the margin between the two. The result is not only increasing malemployment but increasing *un*employment. This was tragically illustrated, for example, in the last months of the German hyperinflation.

Nor can the government mitigate the situation by any such further intervention as "indexing." If it tries to insure, for example, that all workers are paid the average increase that has occurred in wages or prices, it will not only increase wages over the previous average but put out of business even sooner the producers who have not been able, because of lack of demand, to raise their selling prices as much as the average. Every attempt to correct previous distortions and inequities by government ukase will only create worse distortions and inequities. There is no cure but to halt the inflation. This is itself an operation not without its cost, but that cost is infinitely less than that of continuing the inflation—or even of trying to slow it down "gradually."

In sum, an inflation can increase employment only temporarily, only to the extent that it is unexpected, and only when it is comparatively mild and in its early stages. Its long-run effect is to misdirect employment and finally to destroy it. The belief that inflation reduces unemployment is perhaps the most costly myth of the present age.

15

The Specter of "Unused Capacity"

One of the most frequent excuses for inflation is that if a little extra money is printed its effect won't be to raise prices but only to increase the volume of sales and production, because at the moment the new issues of money are being recommended industry is not working at "full capacity."

In the month, say, that the new dose of inflation is being advocated, the official estimates show that industrial plants are working at only 70 or 80 percent of capacity. Therefore, when the new inflation puts more money into the hands of consumers, they will use it to buy more goods. Manufacturers will simply increase their production to meet the increased demand, and prices will not rise until after plants are working at full capacity and cannot increase output further. At that point the issue of new money can simply be stopped.

The writer mainly responsible for the popularity of this theory is John Maynard Keynes. It is akin to the same writer's full-employment argument. It is, in fact, part of the same argument, because for Keynes the supreme economic goal, the *summum bonum*, was the uninterrupted full employment of men and resources.

What the cost of achieving this might be in other respects was simply disregarded.

It may be thought that the criticisms that the present writer and others have already made of the full-employment goal, and of the argument that inflation is the way to achieve it, must apply equally to the full-capacity goal, and therefore need not be repeated. But though the criticisms are of the same general nature, an analysis of the fallacies of the full-capacity goal makes it possible to bring out with much greater sharpness some of the naiveties and errors in the full employment goal as well.

We must begin with a definitional question. What is "full capacity"? The question is seldom raised in popular discussion; but as soon as we examine the problem seriously, we find a wide range of possible definitions. If we think of full capacity from a purely engineering standpoint, then we must think of what could be turned out if factories were operated around the clock, twenty-four hours a day, seven days a week. We would then also have to assume unlimited supplies of labor, with the exact types and mix of skills required, working three or four shifts a week, as well as unlimited supplies of raw materials and other inputs.

A situation like this may be actually possible or desirable in a few industries in wartime or even for a few weeks or months in peacetime, but it would obviously involve mounting problems. Hardly any economist would regard it as an ideal state of affairs.

A second concept of full capacity would envisage maximum output under a "normal" operating schedule, with the customary number of hours per shift and days per week, with downtime for repair and maintenance of machinery. If this concept also assumed high-cost, inefficient facilities brought into production, the resulting output might be defined as the maximum practical capacity. This is the figure commonly used in the official estimates of unused capacity rates.

But this figure refers to potential physical capacity rather than to the optimum rate from an economic standpoint. Few companies want to push their output to the maximum practical level. They would prefer to hold it to the level that achieves maximum long-run profits or other objectives. This involves the assumption that they can obtain all the inputs they need at existing costs per unit and that they can sell unlimited quantities of output at existing prices. It also involves the assumption that they will not be forced into continuous use of their comparatively obsolete equipment. This output level has been called "preferred capacity." [1]

A Department of Commerce study found that for all manufacturers, the preferred operating rate during the period 1965–73 was 94 to 95 percent, considerably above the actual rates.[2]

There are several periodic estimates published of unused manufacturing capacity rates. The two most widely cited are that of the Bureau of Economic Analysis in the Department of Commerce and that of the Federal Reserve Board. There are also a few private estimates, notably those of McGraw-Hill Publications and of the Wharton School at the University of Pennsylvania. All use slightly different methods, The Bureau of Economic Analysis (BEA) obtains its rates by a survey of some 2,400 companies. The respondents generally calculate their utilization rates against maximum practical capacity. It is obvious that each individual answer must itself be an estimate rather than a precisely known figure.

"A Jelly-like Concept"

This is one reason why we cannot depend on the accuracy of the index. As Alan E. Shameer, associate economist of the General Electric Company, put it, "We have dozens of different plants, producing everything from jet engines to plastics to coal to washing machines. How can we possibly say with precision that the company is operating at such-and-such a rate of capacity? . . . It's a jelly-like concept." [3]

If we take the BEA figures of capacity utilization rates for all manufacturers for the eight-year period from December 1965 to December 1973, we find that they ranged from a peak of 87 percent in June 1966 to a trough of 79 percent in September 1970. The difference between the peak and trough rates, in other words, was

---

[1] For a thoughtful discussion of these conceptual and definitional problems, see Marie P. Hertzberg, Alfred I. Jacobs, and Jon E. Trevathan, "The Utilization of Manufacturing Capacity, 1965–73," *Survey of Current Business,* July 1974, pp. 47–57, published by the U.S. Department of Commerce.

[2] *Ibid.,* p. 56.

[3] *Wall Street Journal,* March 11, 1977.

only 8 percentage points. More recent figures tend to show a somewhat wider range. For example, the Federal Reserve Board figure of capacity utilization for all manufacturing in 1974 was 84.2 percent, and in 1975 it was 73.6 percent, a difference of 10.6 percentage points within a single year.

The Fed and BEA figures do not today tend to differ widely; the Fed estimate of average capacity utilization in 1976 was 80.1 percent, and the BEA figure 81.2. But a major effort to improve its past statistics was made recently by the Fed, when it started to take into fuller account, among other things, operations at relatively small companies. The upshot was that factory operations as a whole turned out to be much higher than the Fed originally had supposed. For the 1976 third quarter, for example, the plant-operating figure was boosted sharply to 80.9 percent from the previous 73.6 percent. Perhaps further investigation may result in further revision of the figure, up or down. This once more raises the question of whether the utilization-rate figure is worth using as a "policy-making tool," even if we were to grant that government bureaucrats should ever attempt to "fine-tune" the economy.

When we ask why the cyclical range in the official utilization-rate estimates has not been greater, the main answer is clear. These figures represent the *average* capacity utilization rate of *all* plants in *all* industries. Averages tend always to conceal wide divergence and dispersion. In addition to its overall figure, the BEA gives separate capacity-utilization rates for about a dozen different leading industries. We have seen that the spread between the peak and the trough rates of capacity utilization for all industries from 1965 to 1973 was only 8 percentage points. But the spread in the (nonelectrical) machinery industry was 15, in the rubber industry 22, and in the motor-vehicle industry 42 percentage points.

Even here, however, the real disparities between capacity utilization in different plants and factories were largely concealed because the foregoing figures are again the *average* figures for entire industries, lumping the marginal and the most successful companies together.

To make the real problem clearer, let us suppose that at the moment the average capacity utilization rate for all manufacturing is 80 percent. A Keynesian might then say that if we increased the money supply by 20 percent the result would be stimulating but not inflationary, because this new money would merely supply the

105

purchasing power to buy 20 percent more goods, and industry already happens to have the idle capacity to turn out that much more goods "without inflation" or unwanted price increases.

But suppose this 80 percent average figure, though reasonably accurate, conceals a real situation in which the capacity utilization rate in different plants actually ranges from a low of 60 to a high of 100 percent, with the lowest 11 percent of plants operating at only 60 percent, the next 11 percent segment above that operating at 65 percent, the third segment at 70 percent, and so on, with the ninth and highest segment operating at full capacity.

Supposing the Keynesian scheme otherwise operates in accordance with the schemers' intentions, what would be the result? All factories would be operating, or trying to operate, at a rate 20 percent higher than before. The half that had been operating at less than 80 percent could presumably do this, but the half that had already been operating above that rate would be running into bottlenecks and shortages in plant and equipment, not to speak of the problems of all manufacturers in buying additional specialized input and hiring additional specialized labor. Prices—including wage rates and other costs, which are themselves prices—would begin to soar.

(Of course the neat and even distribution of dispersion that my hypothetical figures suggest would not occur. I have assumed it merely to simplify the arithmetic. But it is important to keep in mind that there is bound to be some such dispersion.)

Our analysis brings out the simplistic and completely unreal nature of the Keynesian assumptions, and of so-called macroeconomics in general. This macroeconomics deals almost exclusively in averages and aggregates. In doing so it falsifies causation and neglects individual processes, individual industries, individual companies, individual prices, and the immense diversity of services and products.

The Keynesian Heaven

The Keynesian economic heaven is apparently one in which there is constant full employment of men and plant and equipment. Nobody and no machine is temporarily idle because the economy is in transition. The balance and proportions among the thousands of individual industries and products remain constantly the same. No industry is contracting and laying off help because of declining demand for its particular product, and therefore no capital and labor can be released so that other industries can expand. No processes, machines, or plant become obsolete because of new methods or new inventions, and therefore never have to be shut down, idled, or scrapped. Every industry is apparently turning out a homogeneous and unchanging product, and can hire additional workers from a sort of homogeneous labor pool. There is no such thing as a surplus or shortage of specialized skills. Unemployment is solely the result of "insufficient purchasing power," and can be remedied simply by increasing that purchasing power.

Not only could such an economy exist only in some never-never land, but no serious economist could regard it as desirable. It is the result of turning full employment and full utilization of capacity, which are merely means, into the overriding economic end.

Let us turn our attention to a few actual consequences of Keynesian policies that the Keynesians chronically overlook.

They assume that an increased money and credit supply—as long as there is not full employment and the economy is not operating at full capacity—will not lead to increased wage rates or increased prices because industry will simply hire previously idle labor and turn out more goods to take care of the increased demand.

This assumption neglects two factors. The first is that average or overall unemployment and average or overall unused capacity are not what count. The percentage of unemployment is different in every industry and locality, and the percentage of unused capacity is different in every plant. When general or special demand increases, shortages will quickly occur at particular localities of workers with special skills, and bottlenecks will soon develop in individual industries, factories, and plants. Capacity is reached when we have fully employed our most scarce resource or complementary productive factor, whether that is an important key industry, specialized labor, plant, or some raw material. When this situation occurs the price of the scarce factor or factors will begin to soar, and this rise will soon force increases in other wage rates and prices.

There is a second overlooked factor. Even if the distribution of both unemployed labor and unused capacity were uniform, increased demand would in any case promptly bring a rise of wage rates and prices. Intelligent speculators (and every businessman and even every consumer must be to some extent a speculator) do not wait until there is an actual shortage of anything before they start bidding up prices; they do this as soon as they foresee the probability or the possibility of a shortage. And the greater the probability seems, the higher they bid. Every successful businessman tends to be successful in proportion to his ability to *anticipate* a change in conditions, to buy or sell before his competitors or the general public are aware of the coming situation. It is only the Keynesians' blindness to this everyday fact of business life which leads them to assume and predict that new issues of money will not result in inflation until every man is employed and every factory is going full blast.

Let us come back now to the specific problem of unused plant capacity. The Keynesians seem to assume that it is both possible and desirable for all plants to work continuously at full capacity. It is neither. The demand for all sorts of products—motor boats, snowplows and lawnmowers, skis and roller skates, overcoats and bathing suits—is seasonal. For that or other reasons, their production tends to be seasonal (even though the output season precedes the selling season). In order that there may be sufficient production at the peak of the season, there must be at least some unused capacity off-season. The unused capacity does not necessarily mean economic waste; it is its *availability when needed* that counts.

For the same reason, when a firm's plant has been working at full capacity for more than a short period, it is probably a sign that the firm has missed an economic opportunity. It should have foreseen this situation and expanded its plant or built a new one to meet the increased demand for its product. Producers do, in fact, constantly try to do just this. It has long been recognized that in periods of low operating rates industry does not tend to expand, but that as operating rates increase, there is an increase of investment in new plant. Businessmen recognize that they must normally accept some "surplus" capacity in order to be sure they will have enough when they need it. Not only is it unprofitable for them to be fully using their more obsolescent plants and machines, but they should be periodically replacing them with the most modern and

108

efficient equipment. In brief, the most desirable normal situation for the individual plant owner or manager is one in which there is at least some "unused" capacity.

Investment Discouraged

In a recent penetrating study,[4] however, M. Kathryn Eickhoff, vice-president and treasurer of Townsend-Greenspan and Company, pointed out that from 1970 until the date her study was made, increased plant operating rates were not leading to investment in new plant as early as they previously did. The "trigger point" that set off new investment seemed to be moving to higher and higher operating rates. That trigger point in 1977 seemed to be an average capacity utilization rate of approximately 87 percent. This was ominous, because the highest rate in the preceding recovery was 87.6 percent·during 1973, the year the nation moved into double-digit inflation.

What this meant, among other things, was that increased issues of money and credit were tending to lead to output shortages sooner than previously, and therefore were leading to sharper and higher price rises sooner than previously.

Miss Eickhoff also presented an acute analysis of the reasons why inflation and inflationary expectations increase uncertainty and thereby discourage new investment. The greater the uncertainty in the business outlook, she pointed out, the greater becomes the rate of return required for new investment to compensate for that uncertainty, and the fewer the number of projects which will qualify. Inflation, especially when it is expected to accelerate, always increases business uncertainty. Even if overall profits advance in line with the rate of inflation, no single producer can be sure that his profits will rise to the same extent. That will depend upon how much his costs rise relative to all other prices in the economy, and whether or not he can raise his prices correspondingly. As a result, the dispersion of profits among producers increases as the rate of inflation climbs. This dispersion of profits does far more to dis-

---

[4] "Plant vs. Equipment Considerations in the Capital Goods Outlook," presentation before the Cleveland Business Economists Club, February 2, 1977.

courage investment than the prospect of an overall increase of profits does to induce it. In effect, a much higher rate of future discount is applied to inflation-generated profits than to those resulting from normal business operations.

Thus the inflation that the Keynesians and others advocate in order to stimulate employment, production, and investment ends by discouraging, deterring, and diminishing all three.

16

Inflation versus Profits

One of the reasons why inflation is persistently advocated by Keynesians and others is that it is thought to increase the profitability of business. This is, in fact, an essential part of the argument of those who believe that inflation tends to bring full employment. By improving the outlook for profits, it leads enterprises to start new businesses or to expand old businesses, and therefore to take on more workers.

As we have seen, inflation may sometimes actually have this effect in its early stages. If it raises final selling prices more than it raises wages and other costs, and if it is expected to be only a temporary condition, it can stimulate increased investment and increased production. But when the inflation continues and is expected to continue, people begin to make compensating adjustments. Wages, interest rates, raw material prices, and other costs begin to go up as fast as or faster than final retail prices. Profit margins begin to narrow or to become increasingly uncertain for individual firms. The "stimulus" of inflation becomes a deterrent.

There is an additional factor. Businessmen begin to discover that their monetary profits have been to a certain extent illusory. The dollar profits shown on their income accounts are misleading, be-

111

cause the dollar does not have the purchasing power it previously had.

Economists and statisticians have been aware of this at least ever since index numbers of prices began to be compiled, but it is only in recent years that the accounting profession has acknowledged and attempted to do something to meet the problem.

Accounting reform has been rather piecemeal. It began around 1936. One of the principal practices that falsified financial accounts in an inflationary period was the orthodox method of dealing with inventories. The accountant assumed that the raw materials or parts that were bought earliest were those that were used first and embodied in the final product first. This was called the "first-in, first-out" assumption (FIFO). If a part at the time of acquisition cost one dollar, and at the time of the sale of the finished product cost two dollars, the manufacturer in effect showed an added profit on his books equivalent to one dollar on each of those parts. But this was a "phantom" profit, not likely to be repeated, because when he came to replace that part it would cost him two dollars.

So accountants are now increasingly advocating the use of the "last-in, first-out" method of inventory accounting (LIFO). The latest price paid for a particular item of inventory is the price used in making up the account. This means in effect that withdrawals from inventory are priced at the current price paid for additions to inventory. So on the assumption that inventory volume and production rates are relatively constant, LIFO removes part of the phantom profit shown by inflation. Even at the time of writing, however, the firms taking advantage of the LIFO method of inventory accounting are still in a minority.

A second problem to be recognized by accountants is the amount of write-off that a firm must make every year for the depreciation and obsolescence of its plant and equipment. Here again firms in the past have been grossly overestimating and overstating their profits in an inflationary period by making an insufficient write-off for depreciation.

Let us say that a firm's plant originally cost it $1 million and its equipment another $1 million, and that it depreciates its plant on a "straight-line" basis over a forty-year period and its equipment over a ten-year period. Then each year, on the average, it will be writing off $25,000 of its plant investment and $100,000 of its equipment investment against its gross earnings. But suppose at the end of the ten-year period it finds that to replace its equipment

112

costs it $2 million, and that at the end of the forty-year period to replace its plant will cost it $16 million (with prices doubling every ten years). Then even at the end of ten years the $125,000 that it has deducted annually will prove to have been grossly inadequate. It may find that it has been paying dividends out of phantom profits, that is, out of capital. At the end of the forty-year period, or much earlier, it may find itself unable to continue in business.

To solve this problem, some accountants are now proposing that depreciation allowances in an inflation no longer be based on original cost of equipment but on replacement cost. This, however, raises other questions. How should the replacement cost be calculated? Should it be the cost of replacing the identical plant or equipment, or the cost of an asset of equivalent operating or productive capability? It is obvious that this calculation is going to involve a lot of subjective guesswork. Still another problem is that in a continuing inflation it is impossible to allow accurately on an annual basis for replacement costs until the year that actual specific replacements have to be made.

Still another accounting problem in an inflation is how to calculate interest charges. Much depends on whether a company is a net lender or a net borrower. If it is a net borrower, it will probably pay during an inflation a higher than normal interest rate for money. On the other hand, it will be paying back its debt in money of depreciated purchasing power as compared with when it was borrowed. It is probable that its "real" gain from this depreciation will be greater than its "real" loss from a higher interest rate.

The Bottom Line

We come, finally, to "the bottom line." After all allowances have been made to put inventories, depreciation, and other costs on a "real" rather than on a money basis, we come to the amount of net profit. But when we compare this with preceding years we have to remember that the dollars shown in the net profit figure have not the same purchasing power as the dollars shown in the net profit of earlier years.

The ideal of "rational accounting" in an inflation can only be achieved if we can eliminate fluctuations due to changes in the average purchasing power of money and restate everything in terms of dollars of constant purchasing power—all adjusted to some single base year or base period. But this is not easy to do. We will get different results if, for example, in resorting to official calculations, we use the GNP implicit price deflator or the consumer price index to make our adjustments.

Let us put aside pure theory for the moment, and ask what the actual effect has been of using or not using the new inflation-accounting rather than orthodox methods. The difference has not been trivial. In 1973, the economists of Morgan Guaranty Trust Company calculated that for the second quarter of 1973 phantom profits accounted for 40 percent of the total profits reported—$21.1 billion out of a total annual level of $51.9 billion. In September 1975 George Terborgh presented a table of profits of nonfinancial corporations for each of the eleven calendar years 1964 through 1974, based on Department of Commerce data. Here are his figures for 1974 (in billions of dollars): profits before taxes as reported, $110.1; income tax liability, $45.6; profits after taxes as reported, $64.5; understatement of costs (because of failure to use inflation accounting), $48.4; profits before tax as adjusted, $61.7; profits after tax as adjusted, $16.1; dividend payments, $26.2; adjusted retained earnings, *minus* $10.1. In other words, in 1974 these corporations thought they were earning and reported they were earning $64.5 billion after taxes. But they were really earning only $16.1 billion after taxes. And of the $26 billion that they paid out in dividends, more than $10 billion came out of capital.[1]

Later figures confirm this result. Alcan Aluminum, with conventional accounting, posted a respectable pretax profit of $96 million for 1976. But required by the Securities and Exchange Commission to assume that its plants and inventories were to be replaced at 1977's inflated prices, Alcan discovered that its allowances for depreciation soared 140 percent and its cost of sales edged up 2 percent. As a result of subtituting this replacement-cost accounting, Alcan's $96 million pretax profit became a hypothetical $119 million loss. This was an extreme case, but some of the profit reductions shown by other large companies were almost as striking.[2]

Apart from all other difficulties, vested interests stand in the way

---

[1] *Capital Goods Review* (Washington, D.C.: Machinery and Allied Products Institute, September 1975).

[2] *Wall Street Journal*, May 23, 1977.

of "scientific" accounting. Even government agencies are in conflict. On the one hand, the Securities and Exchange Commission wants a company to make adjustments for inflation so as not to give investors an exaggerated idea of its profitability. On the other hand, the Internal Revenue Service would like to collect the maximum tax possible, and thus would like all accounts on an orthodox dollar basis. There is a similar conflict of interest in private business. The owner or stockholders of a company would like things to be on an inflation-accounting basis so as to pay the minimum tax to the government. But the hired managers of the business would like to show the highest profits as a proof of their good management—not to speak of the fact that many of them receive salary bonuses based on conventionally calculated profits per share.

Increasing Uncertainty

Putting aside all questions of vested interest, it is increasingly difficult for a corporation to know, during a prolonged period of severe inflation, what it is actually earning. If it keeps conventional accounts, showing costs on a historical dollar basis, it will get false results and appear to be earning more than it is. But if it attempts to adjust for the rise in prices over time, its adjustments may also be misleading. If, for example, the prices of its specific inventories have gone up more than the average rise in the wholesale or consumer price index, the difference, when those specific inventories have been used up, will represent a "real" profit. And if the managers attempt to allow for quality differences in replaced inventories or plant and equipment, their accounts will again reflect subjective guesswork.[3]

To emphasize the ambiguity of replacement-cost concepts, the U.S. Steel Corporation, for example, noted that its 1976 replacement cost depreciation would be $600 million under one set of

---

[3] George Terborgh has persuasively argued that in converting historical accounting entries into their present-day equivalents it is better both for theoretical and for practical reasons to use only a *single* index reflecting changes in the *general* purchasing power of the dollar, and not to attempt to adjust for the specific price rises in items of inventory or equipment. See *The Case for the Single-Index Correction of Operating Profit* (Washington, D.C.: Machinery and Allied Products Institute, 1976).

assumptions but would range from $1.1 billion to $1.3 billion under another. Some other companies found that though their replacement cost would be much higher than the historical cost of their plant and equipment, they would be replacing with far more efficient equipment. As a result, industries with rapidly improving technology find their hypothetical profit results much less affected by inflation accounting than industries with a stagnant technology.[4]

That corporation managers and investors in an inflationary period will not know precisely how much their companies are earning is not a matter of merely academic interest. It is chiefly by comparing profitability that men decide what business to go into, or, if they are irrevocably in a given business, in which particular items to increase production and in which to reduce it.

Inflation changes the profitability, or apparent profitability, of different businesses and occupations, and so leads to extensive changes in what is produced. When a major inflation is over, it is discovered that it has led in many cases to increased production of the wrong things at the cost of more necessary things. It leads to malproduction and malinvestment, and hence to huge waste.

But still another effect becomes increasingly serious. Not only do investors and managers not know what their companies are currently earning; they know still less what they are going to earn in the future. In the face of all experience, one of the most persistent of all fallacies is the tacit assumption that in an inflation all prices and wages rise at the same rate. This fallacy is nourished by the monthly publication of official index numbers reducing all wholesale and consumer prices to a single average, and by the persistent newspaper headlines citing "the" rate of inflation. These government averages of 400 to 2,700 different prices tend to make the man on the street, and even many professional economists, forget that even in normal times all individual prices are constantly changing in relation to each other, and that in periods of severe inflation this diversity and dispersion of price movements becomes far greater.

As we have seen elsewhere, all this leads to increasing business uncertainty. Even if, on the average, inflation tends to increase the total of dollar profits, no individual businessman knows how it is going to affect his own firm. He does not know how much his

---

[4] *Wall Street Journal*, May 23, 1977.

particular costs—for equipment, raw materials, and labor—are going to rise relative to all other prices in the economy, or whether or not he will be able to raise his own prices correspondingly. This disparity and dispersion of profits among producers increases as the rate of inflation climbs. The increasingly uncertain incidence of profits does far more to discourage new investment than the prospect of an overall increase of profits does to encourage it. A much higher rate of future discount is applied to inflation-generated profits than to those resulting from normal business operations. So employment, production, and investment are not only misdirected by inflation; in the long run they are all discouraged and diminished.[5]

---

[5] In addition to the two papers by George Terborgh cited in the text, the reader interested in pursuing the accounting problem in more detail is referred to James H. Sadowski and Mark E. Nadolny, *Inflation Accounting* (*The Arthur Anderson Chronicle,* January 1977), and Solomon Fabricant, *Toward Rational Accounting in an Era of Unstable Money* (New York: National Bureau of Economic Research, Report 16, December 1976). Fabricant's discussion is not only excellent in itself but appends references to some forty other publications on the subject.

17

Inflation and Interest Rates

One of the persistent causes of inflation is the perennial demand for cheap money. The chronic complaint of businessmen, and still more of politicians, is that interest rates are too high. The popular complaint is directed especially against the rate for home mortgages.

To cite an example at random, President Lyndon B. Johnson, in his State of the Union message in January 1967, "pledged" to the American people to "do everything in the President's power to lower interest rates and to ease money." Whether he knew it or not, this was a pledge to resume and increase inflation.

But it is not merely by presidential pledges that governments seek to hold down interest rates arbitrarily. Since the passage of the Federal Reserve Act in 1913, government efforts and power to hold down interest rates have been built into our monetary system.

The Federal Reserve authorities have three specific powers to enable them to do this. The first is the power to set the discount rate—the rate at which the member banks can borrow from the Reserve banks. The second is the power to change the reserve requirements of the member banks. The third is the power to purchase government securities in the open market.

The first of these powers helps set short-term interest rates directly. When member banks can freely borrow money from their Federal Reserve bank at, say, 6 percent, this fixes a ceiling on the rate they have to pay. They can afford to relend at any rate above that. In classical central bank theory, the discount rate was treated as a penalty rate. In the nineteenth century, the Bank of England, for example, set its discount rate slightly *above* the rate at which the private banks lent to their own customers with highest credit standing. If a private bank then got into difficulties and had to borrow from the Bank of England, putting up some of the loans due to it as security, it lost by the operation. The discount rate was not supposed to enable a private bank to relend its borrowings from the Bank of England at a profit. But in this inflationary age, that rule has long been forgotten. Most countries today fix their central bank discount rate (sometimes called the rediscount rate) at a level *below* what the private banks charge even their highest-rated customers.

But there are limitations to prevent a low official discount rate from being too greatly abused as an incentive to inflation. Not only are severe "eligibility" restrictions often put on the kind and term of commercial paper that the member banks are allowed to rediscount, but the would-be member bank borrower may be subjected to embarrassing questioning, and the "discount window" may in effect be kept all but closed. In October 1976, for example, when the Federal Reserve banks were holding $100,374 million in U.S. government securities and extending total credits of $107,312 million, only $67 million of this consisted of loans to member banks.

The second power of the Federal Reserve authorities—the power to lower the reserve requirements of the member banks—could be used to allow the member banks to expand their loans, but in practice the reserve requirement is seldom changed. The required reserve against net demand deposits for "central-reserve city" member banks, for example, stood unchanged at 13 percent from 1917 to 1935. From January 1, 1963, it stood for years at about 16.5 percent. The formula is now somewhat complicated, but not essentially different. There are quicker and more flexible ways to obtain a desired expansion of the money supply.

The chief way is by the power of the Federal Reserve authorities to purchase government securities in the open market. This power is employed almost daily. It is easy to see how it expands the

119

supply of money and credit. A Federal Reserve bank buys, say, $1 billion of U.S. government securities in the open market. It buys them, say, from private holders, and pays for them with a cashier's check. The sellers deposit their checks in some commercial bank, dominantly in a member bank. The member banks present their checks to the Reserve bank for payment. As a result, their "reserve balances" with the Reserve bank increase $1 billion.

Let us say that the member banks are already "lent up," that is, that they have already expanded their loans as much as they are allowed to do against their legally required minimum reserves. They now have $1 billion of "excess reserves," and they are entitled to lend out at least three or four times this amount, the exact multiple depending on how much the borrowers draw out in actual cash. So Federal Reserve bank purchases of every $1 billion of government securities can lead to an expansion of the money and credit supply by some $3–4 billion.

The power of the Federal Reserve System to expand the money supply in this fashion is used daily and heavily. In 1975 the Fed banks made gross purchases of $20,892 million in U.S. government securities (mostly—$11,562 million—Treasury bills with maturities of twelve months or less) and gross sales of $5,599 million. In recent years the system's total holdings of government securities have tended constantly to increase—from $57,500 million in December 1969, for instance, to $105,682 million in December 1977.

How Rates Are Reduced

So the government can bring about lower interest rates, in the first instance, by two methods. It can do it directly by reducing the discount rate of the central bank and allowing private banks to borrow freely at that rate. Or it can do it indirectly by "increasing the supply of loanable funds"—that is, by inflating. It can inflate in this way through getting the central bank to purchase its bonds, or it can "monetize" its debt directly—that is, it can just print the money to pay for what it buys. The latter process, however, is too naked, too raw, too clearly seen through, and no respectable government today resorts to it. Modern governments prefer the more complicated method I have described above, because the majority of voters (and even some of the politicians) are only dimly aware of precisely what is being done.

In sum, if we directly lower the interest rate, we encourage more borrowing and therefore encourage an increase in the money-and-credit supply. If we begin by increasing the money-and-credit supply, we thereby lower the interest rate. So one begets the other: lower interest rates bring about inflation, and inflation brings about lower interest rates.

But there is a catch that the inflationists and easy money advocates do not foresee. The second effect is at best temporary. Inflation brings about lower interest rates only in the short run. In the longer run inflation brings about higher interest rates than ever, for inflation, by raising prices, lowers the purchasing power of the monetary unit. Lenders begin to catch on to this. They want a real return, say, of 5 percent a year. But in the preceding year prices rose an average of 6 percent. If prices continue to rise at that rate, it will take a nominal return of something like 11 percent to bring a real return of 5 percent. So lenders begin to demand a "price premium" sufficient to insure themselves of something close to their normal return.

The current nominal interest rate demanded and offered is therefore determined by the composite expectations of lenders and borrowers concerning the future rate of inflation. These expectations, in turn, are largely influenced by the past and present rate of inflation. Experience shows that these expectations, in the early stages of inflation, tend to lag greatly behind what the future rate actually turns out to be.

For a long time officialdom, in particular, tries to ignore the situation completely. Thus in the raging German hyperinflation of 1919–23 the Reichsbank kept its official rate unchanged at 5 percent until June 22, 1922, and even then began raising it only one percentage point a month till practically the end of the year. In 1923 it began to pay more attention to reality. It was charging 90 percent in September of that year and 900 percent after that. But it never did catch up with reality. At the beginning of November 1923 the *market* rate for "call money" rose as high as 30 percent per day, or more than 10,000 percent on an annual basis.

I have earlier pointed out that the classical (or at least the late nineteenth century) British theory and practice of the discount rate placed it *above* the rate that the private banks were charging their own best customers for loans. The rediscount privilege was ostensibly granted to the private banks only for emergency use. It would be restricted to such use, it was assumed, if the banks paid a penalty rate for what they were forced to borrow. But when our own Federal Reserve banks began to operate in 1914, they soon began to set the discount rate below the market rate under the influence of political pressure and an easy-money ideology. The rate of the New York Federal Reserve Bank was set at 6 percent in 1914, but was down to 4 percent by 1917. In the Depression, from 1933 to 1935, it was held under 2 percent, falling to the incredibly low rate of 1 percent between 1937 and 1946. Even in August 1958, though prices were rising in that year and the purchasing power of the dollar had already fallen to only about forty-eight cents compared with 1939, the discount rate was set at only 1.75 percent.

Other leading central banks throughout the world followed much the same easy-money policies. The discount rate almost everywhere became a national show-window rate; it bore little relation to the high market rates that the majority of businessmen were actually obliged to pay.

But the central banks have lately been forced to pay some attention to these realities. We get an instructive table if we put together two separate tables in the December 1976 issue of *International Financial Statistics,* published by the International Monetary Fund. Our combined table compares, for thirteen industrial countries, the average annual yields (if held to maturity) of central government bonds of at least twelve years' life, with the respective discount

	Long-Term Bond Yield	Discount Rate
United States	6.65%	5.50%
Canada	9.09	9.50
Japan	8.71	6.50
Belgium	9.11	9.00
Denmark	13.83	11.00
France	9.63	10.50
Germany	7.80	3.50
Italy	13.36	15.00
Netherlands	9.08	7.00
Norway	7.22	6.00
Sweden	9.15	8.00
Switzerland	4.60	2.00
United Kingdom	16.03	15.00

rates of the central banks of those countries. The figures are mainly those for October 1976.

Thus it will be seen that though the short-term discount rate is below the long-term government bond yield in ten of these countries, there is in general a remarkable correspondence between the two rates in nearly all the countries. The very high nominal discount rates in Italy and the United Kingdom reflect the high nominal long-term rates that then prevailed in those countries. And both were so high because the rates embodied the price premium that lenders demanded because they expected future inflation rates approximately equal to recent past inflation rates.

Where there has recently been hyperinflation, discount rates have been forced to reflect this, at least in part. In October 1976 the discount rate in Brazil was 28 percent and in Colombia 20 percent. In Chile the discount rate rose from 15 percent in 1971 to 20 percent in 1972 and 50 percent in 1973. In the first quarter of 1974 it was raised to 75 percent, after which it ceased to be reported.

A review of past inflation records reveals that though interest rates eventually rise to reflect expectations of future price rises, they tend for an astonishingly long time to lag behind the rate that would have been sufficient to protect the lender and give him a customary real yield. This lag persists because it seems to take a long period for lenders to abandon their habit of thinking only of the nominal yield from their investments. To protect themselves they must consider, instead, the real yield to them after allowing for inflation. They must adequately estimate the extent of future inflation during the life of their loan. As a result of failure to do this, they frequently find that they have accepted a negative real interest rate.

Consequences of Manipulation

This was illustrated in an instructive article by Ernest J. Oppenheimer in *Barron's* (August 30, 1976). "Ever since the New Deal," he charged, "the Federal government has pursued a deliberate policy of manipulating interest rates in favor of borrowers, notably itself."

He presented a table covering the thirty-six years from 1940 to 1975 inclusive. This listed in four separate columns (1) the actual yields in each year of three-month U.S. Treasury bills and of long-term government bonds, (2) the "annual inflation rate" (i.e., the price rise each year), (3) the "assumed normal yield" (i.e., the yield that would have been sufficient to compensate the holder if it were to offset the "inflation" rate and in addition give the holder a real yield of 2 percent from his Treasury bills and 3 percent from his bonds), and (4) a calculation of the "real" gain or loss to the investor in that year.

The table revealed that on this calculation the investor in U.S. Treasury bills lost money in all but six years, and the investor in long-term bonds lost money in all but three years of the thirty-six year period. The interest payments these investors received during the whole period were not even sufficient to offset what they lost through inflation.

Summarizing what happened in 1975 alone, Oppenheimer wrote, "Altogether, in 1975 the Federal government paid $31 billion interest on its $577 billion total indebtedness. Just to cover the inflation rate of 9.14 per cent [that year] would have required $52.7 billion. Thus investors in government securities lost over $21 billion on inflation in one year, not to mention any return on capital."

It is important to keep in mind, however, that these investor losses were not directly the result of government manipulation of interest rates. This manipulation caused the losses only insofar as it helped to cause the inflation. The buyers of all fixed-return securities, private as well as government, suffered similar real losses during the same thirty-six years. What the buyers paid for these securities was the market rate at the time, but the market rate (except in rare cases) proved insufficient to compensate them. The cure is not, as Oppenheimer seems at one point to suggest, that the government (or any other borrower) should offer to compensate the lender for any inflation-loss actually suffered. That would be ruinous to most borrowers. The cure—for this as well as a score of other evils—is simply to halt inflation.

After an inflation finally comes to an end, in fact, the high nominal interest rates eventually brought about by the inflation tend to continue; and then they give the lender far more than the customary real yield. This was illustrated in Germany during and after the hyperinflation of 1919–23. While interest rates never caught up with the rate of price increase until the very end, in April and May 1924—five to six months after the inflation was over—monthly

124

loans in Berlin were receiving interest equivalent to 72 percent a year.

The pure rate of interest is not a merely monetary phenomenon. It reflects what is called time-preference. It means the discount of future goods as against present goods. It helps to determine the proportions in which money is spent and saved, the times and proportions in which consumption goods are made and capital goods are made. It acts as a guide to which projects are likely to be profitable and which not. It helps to determine the entire allocation and pattern of output.

Because inflation leads inevitably to distortions in the interest rate, because during it nobody knows what future prices, costs, or price-cost relations are likely to be, it inevitably distorts and unbalances the structure of production. It gives rise to multitudinous illusions. Because the nominal interest rate, though it rises, does not rise enough, funds are more heavily borrowed than before; uneconomic ventures are encouraged; corporations making high nominal profits invest abnormal sums in expansion of plant. Many regard this, when it is happening, as a happy byproduct of inflation. But when the inflation is over much of this investment is found to have been misdirected—to have been malinvestment, sheer waste. And when the inflation is over, also, there is found to be, because of this previous misdirection of investment, a real and sometimes intense capital shortage.

18

How Cheap Money Fails

John Maynard Keynes preached two great remedies for unemployment. One was deficit financing. The other was artificially cheap money brought about by central bank policy. Both alleged remedies have since been assiduously pursued by nearly all governments. The result has been worldwide inflation and a constantly shrinking purchasing power of monetary units. But the success in curing unemployment has been much more doubtful. In an earlier chapter we considered the unpromising results of budget deficits. Does cheap money have any better record?

The following table covers the twelve years 1929–40, comparing the average annual rate of prime commercial paper maturing in four to six months with the percentage of unemployment in the same year. Both sets of figures are from official sources.

In sum, over this period of a dozen years low interest rates did *not* eliminate unemployment. On the contrary, unemployment actually *increased* in years when interest rates went down. Even in the seven-year period from 1934 through 1940, when the cheap-money policy was pushed to an average infralow rate below one percent (0.77 of one percent), an average of more than seventeen in every hundred persons in the labor force were unemployed.

Let up skip over the war years when war demands, massive

Year	Commercial Paper Rate	Percentage of Unemployment
1929	5.85 %	3.2 %
1930	3.59	8.7
1931	2.64	15.9
1932	2.73	23.6
1933	1.73	24.9
1934	1.02	21.7
1935	0.75	20.1
1936	0.75	16.9
1937	0.94	14.3
1938	0.81	19.0
1939	0.59	17.2
1940	0.56	14.6

deficits, and massive inflation combined to bring overemployment, and take up the record again for the eleven years 1949–59.

The following table shows that, although the commercial paper interest rate in this period averaged 2.48 percent—more than three times as high as that in the seven years from 1934 through 1940—

Year	Commercial Paper Rate	Percentage of Unemployment
1949	1.49 %	5.5 %
1950	1.45	5.0
1951	2.16	3.0
1952	2.33	2.7
1953	2.52	2.5
1954	1.58	5.0
1955	2.18	4.0
1956	3.31	3.8
1957	3.81	4.3★
1958	2.46	6.8
1959	3.97	5.5

★ Unemployment percentages before 1957 are based on Department of Commerce "old definitions" of unemployment; for 1957 and after they are based on the "new definitions," which make unemployment slightly higher—4.2 percent of the labor force in 1956, for example, instead of the 3.8 percent in the table.

the rate of unemployment was not higher, but much lower, averaging only 4.4 percent compared with 17.7 percent in the 1934–40 period.

Within this second period, the relationship of unemployment to interest rates is almost the exact opposite of that suggested by Keynesian theory. In 1949, 1950, and 1954, when the commercial paper interest rate averaged about 1.5 percent, unemployment averaged 5 percent and more. In 1956, 1957, and 1959, when commercial paper rates were at their highest average level of the period at 3.70 percent, unemployment averaged only 4.4 percent of the working force.

We come to the next ten-year segment, 1960 through 1969:

Year	Commercial Paper Rate	Percentage of Unemployment
1960	3.85 %	5.5 %
1961	2.97	6.7
1962	3.26	5.5
1963	3.55	5.7
1964	3.97	5.2
1965	4.38	4.5
1966	5.55	3.8
1967	5.10	3.8
1968	5.90	3.6
1969	7.83	3.5

In the ten-year period 1960–69 interest rates were edging up. They averaged 4.64 percent a year, compared with 2.48 percent a year in the 1949–59 period—an increase of 87 percent. Yet the average unemployment rate advanced from 4.4 to only 4.8 percent, or less than 10 percent. And in 1969 itself, when the commercial paper rate was the highest of any year in the period, the unemployment rate was also the lowest for any year in the period.

Now we come to the final seven years:

Year	Commercial Paper Rate	Percentage of Unemployment
1970	7.72 %	4.9 %
1971	5.11	5.9
1972	4.69	5.6

Year	Commercial Paper Rate	Percentage of Unemployment
1973	8.15%	4.9%
1974	9.87	5.6
1975	6.33	8.5
1976	5.35	7.7

Here at last, on the overall figures of these seven years, we seem to find some statistical support for the thesis that high interest rates breed higher unemployment. The average annual commercial paper rate for the period jumped to 6.74 percent, and the average annual unemployment rate also rose—to 6.2 percent. But the briefest analysis shows that even this slight appearance of statistical support is illusory. For if out of this seven years we take the three years—1970, 1973, and 1974—in which interest rates were *above* the average for the period, we find that the average unemployment rate for those three years was only 5.13 percent, or *below* the average for the full period. In the other four years, when interest rates were *lower* than the average for the full period, the average unemployment rate was 6.92 percent—*higher* than for the full period. (In 1977, not shown on the table, the commercial paper rate rose to 5.60 percent, but the unemployment rate fell to 7.0 percent.)

But there may well be an apparent correspondence between higher interest rates and higher unemployment in the future, on the assumption that the present inflation continues or accelerates. The reason is that in the late stages of an inflation interest rates finally begin to catch up with money-depreciation rates, and in the late stages of an inflation, also, the increasing uncertainty and price-cost discoordination breeds increasing unemployment.

In sum, neither deficit spending nor cheap-money policies are enough by themselves to eliminate even prolonged mass unemployment, let alone to prevent unemployment altogether.

The only real cure for unemployment is precisely the one that the Keynsians and inflationists reject—the adjustment of wage rates to the marginal labor productivity, or "equilibrium," level—the balance and coordination of wages and prices. When individual wage rates are in equilibrium with individual prices, there will tend to be full employment regardless of whether interest rates are "high" or "low." But regardless of how low interest rates are pushed, there will be unemployment where wage rates are too high to permit workable profit margins.

129

19

Indexing: The Wrong Way Out

Inflation is not *caused* by the issuance of too much paper money. Inflation *is* the issuance of too much paper money. Its most conspicuous consequence is to raise prices. But it never raises all prices, wages, and incomes simultaneously or to the same extent. The persons whose wages or incomes it raises least or latest suffer the most from inflation and raise the greatest opposition to it.

Therefore some politicians and economists propose that this be remedied by what they call "indexing" or "indexation." This consists in prescribing that everybody's price, wage, or income be raised as much as the average "level" of prices. This usually means by the same percentage the official consumer price index of the country has gone up.

The mere statement of this proposed remedy suggests some of its difficulties. We must distinguish first of all (though it is surprising how seldom this is done) between *mandatory* and *voluntary* indexing. This country has already adopted a large measure of the latter. According to a calculation made in 1975, the incomes of more than 65 million Americans were indexed: 31.3 million Social Security recipients, 19 million food stamp users, 7 million union members, 4 million aged, blind, and disabled persons on federal aid, and so on—including also members of Congress and thousands of other employees of federal, state, and local governments.[1]

This voluntary or quasi-voluntary indexing does some harm, as I shall later point out, but not nearly as much harm as mandatory indexing. Mandatory indexing is a form of government wage-and-price control. Like any form of price control it is bound to be disruptive. "Standard" price control prescribes *maximum* wages and prices; mandatory indexing prescribes *minimum* wages and prices. Imposing price ceilings brings underproduction and overconsumption of many commodities, causes shortages and leads to rationing. Imposing wage and price floors would lead to massive unemployment and to surpluses of goods that could not be sold at the higher prices.

It is amazing that among the champions of compulsory indexing there are some self-styled free-market economists. Inflation from its very nature does not raise all prices, wage rates, and incomes simultaneously and uniformly but at different times and by different amounts. And during an inflation individual prices, wage rates, and incomes also change in relation to each other, for the same variety of reasons that they do when there is no inflation. But the advocates of indexing see all these changing divergencies not as market fluctuations that accelerate and smooth out a necessary reallocation of production to changes in demand, but as "inequities" that need to be eradicated.

What the advocates of indexing overlook is that in a market system, with division of labor, practically every man's money income is some other man's cost. Therefore indexing not only creates more inequities than it cures, but it tends to disrupt and misdirect production. When wage rates in industry X, which have not yet gone up as much as the average, are suddenly and mandatorily boosted to that level, profit margins in that industry are narrowed or wiped out. One result is bankruptcies of marginal producers and less output. Another result is *not* a higher income for all the previous workers in that industry, but more unemployment. Similar consequences follow when raw material prices or rents are boosted by mandatory indexing. And every upward adjustment to produce "equity" creates the need for other upward adjustments, a never-ending process.

---

[1] *U.S. News and World Report,* August 18, 1975.

One of the great evils of inflation, of course, is that it tends to redistribute wealth and incomes erratically and wantonly. Another consequence is that it leads to the misdirection of labor and investment. But indexing, by arbitrarily altering and falsifying the market signals still further, only tends to increase the misdirection and misallocation of labor and output.

The advocates of indexing appeal to a class interest. What they say in effect is: *You* haven't got your "fair share"; *you* are being cheated, and only indexing will save you. Powerful pressure groups push for a kind of indexing calculated to benefit them at the expense of everybody else. But if they could succeed in their aim, the result in the long run would be damaging to them as well as everybody else. The strong unions, for example, want to keep abreast of increases in the consumer price index as a *minimum*. On top of that they ask for so-called productivity increases, increased pensions, and other guarantees. The result can only be reduced returns to employers, leading at best to less capital formation and slower growth, if not to increased bankruptcies and unemployment.

The newspaper reader is typically led to assume that the official consumer price index, on which most indexing schemes are based, represents all prices of all consumer goods. It is in fact not even designed to do that. Its full official name is the "Consumer Price Index for Urban Wage Earners and Clerical Workers." It covers only 400 items out of the thousands bought and sold by consumers. It is weighted to apply to a particular minority. Its calculation is arbitrary in a score of ways. As a measure of changes in "everybody's" cost of living, it lacks precision. And it necessarily must, because each person's particular "mix" of needs and purchases is individual. The average is never the actual. The average family in the United States has 3.48 members, but there is not a single family with 3.48 members.[2]

No Guarantee of Incomes

But these statistical defects are a comparatively minor objection to indexing. Contrary to the naive assumption of its advocates,

---

[2] The reader interested in a fuller analysis of the defects of the CPI may consult the pamphlet *The Case Against Indexation* by John W. Robbins (Committee for Monetary Research and Education, P.O. Box 1630, Greenwich, CT 06830).

indexing simply cannot be applied evenly all around the circle. It can only fix prices; it cannot guarantee incomes. It can order that wage rates be raised; but it cannot insure that employment will not thereby be reduced. It can order that the price of an item be increased, but it cannot guarantee that the sales of that item will not be diminished.

For another example, let us look at how indexing would affect savings and loan institutions. The government, as has been suggested, could offer notes and bonds on which the annual interest rate varied with consumer prices, and on which even repayment of principal was increased to correspond with consumer price rises. Perhaps some private borrowers would offer similar bonds. In that case there would probably be massive withdrawals from the savings banks to buy such securities. How could the savings banks then maintain their liquidity or solvency? Would they, in order to compete, have to offer their depositors a similarly indexed interest rate and indexed repayment of principal? Where would they get the money from? Would they, in lending mortgages, also demand an indexed interest rate and a similarly scaled-up repayment of principal? How many homeowners would dare to undertake such a risk or be able to meet the terms in the event of a major inflation?

Mandatory indexing is practically certain to favor the interests of the most powerful political groups. In a democracy it would favor primarily the big labor unions. It is naive to suppose, as some of the advocates of indexing do, that in the event of an actual fall in prices, the unions would tolerate a corresponding cut in money wages. Indexing would force wage rates up, and keep them up, on a rachet principle.

Among those whose incomes are already indexed—if not over-indexed—are Social Security recipients. This is having a disturbing political effect. It must tend to remove many of our older citizens as opponents of inflation, and make them complacent about it. If elderly persons and the members of labor unions ever come to assume that they are adequately protected against the ravages of inflation, and may even profit by it, the outlook for restoring balanced budgets and a sound currency will become all but hopeless.

Among those who are already overprotected by indexing are retired federal employees. Lately congressmen have been voting themselves all sorts of catch-up raises. This is the most ironic indexing, and the most ominous of all. If those who are responsible for permitting or producing the inflation are allowed to become also the profiteers from inflation, to whom can we look to end it?

One of the most serious inequities wrought by inflation falls on all those subjected to progressive income taxes and to capital-gains taxes. Inflation keeps pushing them into higher tax brackets. They are called on to pay higher percentage rates even though their real income may not have gone up at all. Many are forced to pay taxes on so-called capital gains when in real terms they may actually have suffered capital losses. If the taxpayer were allowed to recalculate his money income or capital gain in "real" terms, it would remove this flagrant inequity, at the same time as it would take part of the profit out of inflation for the government that was producing it.

In this instance the argument for indexation makes a strong appeal to conservatives. In fact, it might perhaps with as much accuracy be called de-indexing taxes as indexing them. But politically speaking, it would be at best very difficult to get such tax de-indexing except as part of a sweeping indexing program. And such a program would only tend to prolong and increase inflation itself.

How Indexing Accelerates Inflation

Indexing tends to prolong and accelerate inflation for two reasons. It would do this because indexing postpones, diminishes, or removes the worst effects of inflation on influential groups, and so greatly reduces the political opposition to inflation. And it does so also because of its purely mathematical effect. In Phase One, say, indexing would bring all (or most) wages and incomes that were below the average up to the average. But as soon as Phase One had been completed, the average itself would be raised by that increase. This would necessitate a further upward adjustment in Phase Two, and so on. To make the new wage and income levels sustainable at each stage, there would be great political and economic pressure to increase the money supply still further.

The effect is even greater when indexing directly increases government expenditures themselves. It does this most notably, for example, when Social Security payments are indexed. When government expenditures are forced up automatically whenever the consumer price index rises, we have come close to a formula for perpetual inflation.

It should be pointed out that the same sort of result would follow, though on a smaller scale, if tax rates were also indexed or de-indexed so as not to go up with increasing nominal money incomes. This indexation would make tax revenues lower than they would otherwise be, and so tend to increase the deficit—unless the government compensated, as it no doubt would, by openly increasing income tax rates.

Even if indexing did not increase inflation or the political pressures for inflation, it should at least be obvious that it does nothing by itself to reduce or slow down inflation. Even Milton Friedman, one of the strongest advocates of indexing, concedes that "indexing per se will not, in my opinion, do anything to reduce inflation," and even that ". . . widespread indexation would reduce the public pressure to end inflation."[3]

How does it come about that, with all the objections to it, indexing is nonetheless being seriously proposed and discussed? The active discussion began in this country early in 1974, when Milton Friedman returned from a short visit to Brazil full of enthusiasm for the indexing program that he found there.

Brazil as a Model

To have Brazil upheld as an economic or monetary model for the United States to emulate seems a strange irony. Brazil, one must admit, does not have the very worst inflation record in the world in recent years. Chile and Argentina have been competing too vigorously for that honor. But Brazil does have *one* of the worst records—especially one of the worst long-term records. It was inflating at a double-digit rate as early as 1941. The table on page 136 shows its annual record for the last twenty-six years.

It will be noticed that in the single year 1964 consumer prices in Brazil soared 86.6 percent. In fact, in the first quarter of 1964 the annual rate of inflation was running at 150 percent, but at that point the Brazilian authorities took hold and applied the old-fashioned "classical medicine." They imposed a heroic contraction in the growth of "aggregate demand" by severe fiscal and monetary restraint. It was this, and not indexing, that slowed down the cost-of-living rise to just under 25 percent in 1967.

---

[3] Milton Friedman, *Indexing and Inflation* (Washington, D.C.: American Enterprise Institute, 1974), pp. 2, 18.

Annual Consumer Price Rise, Year-end	
1952——20.8%	1965——45.4%
1953——16.8	1966——41.1
1954——26.2	1967——24.5
1955——19.1	1968——24.0
1956——21.7	1969——24.2
1957——13.4	1970——20.9
1958——17.3	1971——18.1
1959——52.0	1972——14.0
1960——23.8	1973——13.7
1961——43.2	1974——32.7
1962——55.2	1975——31.5
1963——80.6	1976——45.0
1964——86.6	1977——43.0

Sources: 1952–73, Getúlio Vargas Foundation. Figures for 1974–77 calculated by author from *International Monetary Statistics,* International Monetary Fund, February 1978.

The indexing that was applied in Brazil in this three-year period was not the kind that its present American advocates are recommending. Brazil's authoritarian government was careful *not* to allow full indexing of labor incomes to rising consumer prices. In this way it was not only able to prevent heavy unemployment, but by diverting a larger proportion of industry's income to profits, it encouraged capital accumulation, plant expansion, and "economic growth." Once fuller indexing came into play after 1967, labor's opposition to inflation diminished, and inflationary policies were resumed.[4]

When an inflation once develops and continues beyond a certain point, indexing arises almost spontaneously and spreads by mutual acceptance as the only way of mitigating an otherwise intolerable situation. This was exemplified in the hyperinflation in Germany in 1922 and 1923. But such indexing should always be voluntary, and flexible enough to adapt itself to special situations. When it is

---

[4] For a more detailed description, see Ronald A. Krieger, "Inflation and the 'Brazilian Solution'," *Challenge,* September–October 1974, pp. 43–52. And for a fascinating history of the incredible monetary mismanagement and chronic inflation in Brazil from the seventeenth century to the present, see Norman A. Bailey, *Brazil as a Monetary Model* (Greenwich, Conn.: Committee for Monetary Research and Education, June 1975).

mandatory and Procrustean, it can only increase economic disruption and create at least as many inequities as it cures.

We come back to the point that one man's price, wage, or income is another man's cost. Inflation is a disguised, haphazard, and iniquitous form of taxation. It is a government-imposed swindle or robbery, and most of us must be swindled or robbed by it. As Professor Hans F. Sennholz has put it:

> If a government resorts to inflation, that is, creates money in order to cover its budget deficits or expands credit in order to stimulate business, then no power on earth, no gimmick, device, trick or even indexation can prevent its economic consequences. If by way of inflation government spends $10 billion in real goods, capital or labor, someone somewhere must forego $10 billion in real resources. It is a fundamental principle of inflation that there must be victims. Indexation may shift the victimization; it cannot prevent it.[5]

One last argument against indexing remains. It is the most important of all, and in itself sufficient. The advocates of indexing tacitly take it for granted that inflation is some mysterious and incurable disease, like cancer; and as it cannot be cured, the best we can do is to live with it and try to mitigate the pain as much as possible. This is a preposterous assumption. Every economist worthy of the name knows precisely what causes inflation and how to stop it. It is caused by a government that insists on spending more than it can or is willing to raise by taxes, a government that recklessly runs chronic deficits and issues more paper money to pay for them. If the politicians responsible for government policy had the will, they could stop inflation almost overnight.

The proponents of indexing blandly suggest that the same government that is creating and prolonging the disease continue to do so but graciously provide us with indexing as a partial pain-killer— or rather, that it shift the pain from some of us to someone else. They propose a complicated and spurious cure and overlook the simple, real, and only one: *Stop the inflation.*

---

[5] Hans F. Sennholz, "Indexing: New Verison of an Old Myth," *Inflation Survival Letter,* July 1, 1974, p. 55.

20

Inflation versus Morality

During every great inflation there is a striking decline in both public and private morality. Let us look at three outstanding historic examples.

The first is the French assignat inflation of 1790–96. The moral consequences of this have been vividly depicted by Andrew Dickson White in his little book, *Fiat Money Inflation in France*, which grew out of a lecture he first delivered in 1876.[1]

With prices soaring and the value of money savings rapidly diminishing, an early effect was the obliteration of thrift. Accompanying this was a cancerous increase in speculation and gambling. Stockjobbing became rife. More and more people began to see the advantages of borrowing and later paying off in depreciated money. A great debtor class grew up whose interest was to keep the inflation going. Workers, finding themselves with less and less real pay in terms of what their wages would buy, while others grew rich by gambling, began to lose interest in steady work. The evaporation of the incomes and savings of the lower and middle classes, and the sudden enrichment of speculators, with their os-

---

[1] Published, with an introduction by the present writer, by the Foundation for Economic Education (Irvington-on-Hudson, N.Y.), 1959.

tentatious luxury, led to mounting social resentment and unrest. Cynicism and corruption set in. Even Mirabeau, who only a few months before had risked imprisonment and even death to establish constitutional government, began secretly receiving heavy bribes. The evidence of the general spread of corruption led to widespread distrust and a loss of faith in patriotism and virtue.

The politicians responsible for the inflation sought to throw the blame, then as now, not only on the "speculators" but on the sellers who were forced to raise their prices. One result was that on February 28, 1793, at eight o'clock in the evening, a mob of men and women in disguise began plundering the stores and shops of Paris. At first they demanded only bread; soon they insisted on coffee, rice, and sugar; at last they seized everything on which they could lay their hands. Hundreds of places were plundered. This was endured for six hours. Finally order was restored only by a grant of seven million francs to buy off the mob. When the plundered merchants had the temerity to protest at the Paris City Hall, they were informed that "shopkeepers were only giving back to the people what they had hitherto robbed them of."

All this was followed by forced loans, price controls, increased resort to the guillotine, repudiation of the currency, and a final turning to a "man on horseback"—Napoleon.

Referring to our own Civil War inflation and the need to return to a sound money, Hugh McCulloch, who served as secretary of the treasury from 1865 to 1868, declared in his annual report of 1867:

> It is corrupting the public morals. It is converting the business of the country into gambling, and seriously diminishing the labor of the country. . . . The kind of gambling which it produces is not confined to the stock and produce boards, but is spreading through our towns into the rural districts. Men are apparently getting rich, while morality languishes and the productive energy of the country is being diminished.
>
> Upon the demoralizing influence of an inconvertible government currency it is not necessary to enlarge. . . . It is not to be expected that a people will be more honest than the government under which they live, and while the government of the United States refuses to pay its

notes according to their tenor, or at least so long as it
fails to make proper effort to do so, it practically teaches
the people the doctrine of repudiation.[2]

It is amazing how closely the French assignat pattern was followed in the great German hyperinflation of 1919–23. We find the
same moral and social retrogression: the discouragement and final
obliteration of thrift; the rise in borrowing and prodigal spending;
the increase in speculation and gambling; the declining application
to steady work; the wanton redistribution of income; the consequent growth of cynicism and corruption, of social unrest, bitter-
ness and hatred, and finally of crime. But the details are worth
closer inspection.[3]

A Vast Expropriation

The inflation was an unsettling and revolutionary influence.
During most of its course, it lowered the real income of the workers; it impoverished the old middle class of investors, and many of
those who had made their fortunes from production; it enriched
a new small class of inflation profiteers whose money came from
speculation. Under the appearance of feverish activity the country
was producing less, and most people were poorer. Goods passed
from one speculator to another, through a long chain of middlemen. Some got rich by speculating in foreign exchange; but savings-bank depositors and bondholders were all but wiped out, and
even most holders of industrial securities ended with barely a
fourth of their original investment. On net balance, in sum, the
main profiteers from the inflation were successful speculators
rather than producers; this implied an important distinction between the new rich and the old rich.

"It is no exaggeration to state," writes Bresciani-Turroni, "that
the depreciation of the currency caused in Germany the vastest
expropriation of some classes of society that has ever been effected
in time of peace."[4] The annihilation of the value of the mark meant
the confiscation of the lender's wealth to the gain of the borrower.

---

[2] *Men and Measures of Half a Century* (New York, 1898), p. 202 ff.,
excerpted.

[3] For a fuller account, see Bresciani-Turroni, *Economics of Inflation*.

[4] *Ibid.*, p. 318.

Landowners, for example, were thus able to free their lands from mortgage. Owners of houses, of course, were able to do the same; but in their case this advantage was usually more than offset by the decline in real rents, which soon did not cover even maintenance expenses, so that many owners were forced to sell.

Pensioners and others who lived on fixed money incomes were reduced to abject poverty. So, in fact, were most of those in the professional and academic classes: students, tutors, writers, artists, scholars. These and similar changes were reflected in the statistics of the condition of children—malnutrition, underweight, rickets. The general mortality rate from pulmonary tuberculosis greatly increased between 1921 and 1923.

Property rights were in fact, if not in form, obliterated. The "revaluation" decrees of February 1924 and July 1925 made only a paltry fractional restitution, and of course could not undo the millions of personal injustices and deprivations suffered while the inflation was in progress.

It is no coincidence that crime rose sharply during the German inflation. On the basis of an 1882 index number of 100, the crime rate, which stood at 117 in 1913, rose to 136 in 1921 and 170 in 1923. It declined again in 1925, when the inflation was over, to 122.

What shall we say of conditions nearly everywhere in 1978? Thanks to Keynesian ideology and spending policies, the universal abandonment of the gold standard, and the workings of the International Monetary Fund, we find inflation in practically every country in the world; and we find a corresponding social unrest, disorder, and moral decay.

The steadily rising crime in this country is an outstanding example. Between 1960 and 1970 our crime rate per 100,000 population increased an average of 8 percent a year, and between 1970 and 1973, 4 percent a year. The total increase between 1960 and 1973 was 120 percent. But crime increase in the last eighteen years has not been confined to the United States; it is reported from most other countries.

Another symptom of moral decay is the increasing frequency of scandal and corruption in government circles. One of the saddest illustrations of this is Great Britain, which during most of the nineteenth and early twentieth centuries stood out among nations for the comparative integrity and incorruptibility of its civil servants and political leaders.

The Causal Chain

The chain of causation, from inflation to corruption to crime, is direct. In a free enterprise system, with an honest and stable money, there is dominantly a close link between effort and productivity, on the one hand, and economic reward on the other. Inflation severs this link. Reward comes to depend less and less on effort and production, and more and more on successful gambling and luck. For some, gambling finally comes to seem too chancy, and corruption or crime a surer path to quick reward.

It is important to remember that inflation by its very origin and nature must involve a redistribution of real incomes. The new money that the government prints goes first of all to special interest groups—to government officials, government contractors (and their employees), pensioners, and various recipients of relief and other appropriations. These groups start to spend the new money when it still retains its former purchasing power. But as they spend it they inevitably raise prices. The last to receive the new money (as one group makes purchases from another) must pay the highest prices.

Those who benefit by inflation, in short, do so, and must do so, at the expense of others. The total losses through inflation must offset the total gains. This creates class or group divisions, in which the victims resent the profiteers from inflation, and in which even the moderate gainers from inflation envy the bigger gainers.

Under inflation, nearly everybody is in fact being subjected to an invisible tax. For if the government in a given year spends, say, $70 billion more than it collects in visible taxes, and merely prints the rest, the public as a whole must be losing the equivalent of this $70 billion in real income. But only a handful of people realize clearly what is going on. The majority tend to blame their plight, not on the government, but on those of their neighbors who appear to be profiteering from the inflation. There is a growing sense that the whole economic system has become radically unjust. "They are stealing from me, and I will steal back."

It is not merely that inflation breeds dishonesty in a nation. Inflation is itself a dishonest act on the part of government, and sets the example for private citizens. When modern governments inflate by increasing the paper-money supply, directly or indirectly, they do in principle what kings once did when they clipped coins. Diluting the money supply with paper is the moral equivalent of diluting the milk supply with water. Notwithstanding all the pious pretenses of governments that inflation is some evil visitation from without, inflation is practically always the result of deliberate governmental policy.

This was recognized by Adam Smith in *The Wealth of Nations,* in a passage that bears repeating:

> When national debts have once been accumulated to a certain degree, there is scarce, I believe, a single instance of their having been fairly and completely paid. The liberation of the public revenue, if it has ever been brought about at all, has always been brought about by a bankruptcy; sometimes by an avowed one, but always by a real one, though frequently by a pretended payment.

The pretended payment was inflation. The U.S. government today is paying off in twenty-two-cent dollars the debts it contracted in 1940. Adam Smith went on:

> The honor of a state is surely very poorly provided for, when, in order to cover the disgrace of a real bankruptcy, it has recourse to a juggling trick of this kind, so easily seen through, and at the same time so extremely pernicious.

21

Can You Beat Inflation?

In nearly every country in the world today the outlook is for continued inflation. The arguments of the sound money champions and limited-government advocates have proved futile against the sophistries of the inflationists and the vested interests of the politicians. The politicians have concluded that they can continue to hold office only as long as they spend more than they tax, as long as they redistribute income, as long as they "soak the rich," as long as they hand out subsidies to a score of pressure groups under the plea of "relieving poverty" and showing "compassion."

For years thoughtful and responsible men have hoped that, when the situation in a given country got bad enough, the inflating "welfare" government would be turned out, or would itself reverse its policies. But the expected time of realizing this hope keeps receding into a more distant future. Where, in this country or that, the inflating socialist government has at last been thrown out, the "conservatives" elected in their place have feared to make any but trivial changes. Millions of people have got used to their food subsidies, or their controlled rents, or their high and prolonged unemployment insurance, or their government-provided jobs, or their escalating "social security" benefits. They have come to accept all these subsidies as rights. The existing government fears that any attempt to remove or reduce them will set off riots. The attitude of the politicians in power becomes increasingly one of *"Après nous, le déluge."*

In this climate, more and more individuals abandon hope of ending inflation by political argument or action, and decide to devote all their energies to trying to save themselves from being ruined by inflation. Some even hope to make a profit out of it. Certainly each of us has a duty to himself and his family to try to minimize the harm that inflation threatens to inflict on his own fortunes.

So let us consider what the most appropriate actions are for one who attempts this.

The first piece of advice is negative. It is to tell him what he should *not* hold. He should hold only enough cash for his more immediate needs. He should sell bonds and other securities that yield only a fixed return. He should not put his money into mortgages or annuities. He should reduce his savings-bank deposits to a minimum.

This advice is especially important if he expects a hyperinflation. In the German inflation of 1919–23, prices went up hundreds of billions of times. The value of cash and savings-bank deposits was wiped out. But if he expects only a moderate inflation, our negative advice may not strictly apply. For example, if an inflation (in the sense of an average price-increase) is expected to run at a rate of only 5 percent a year, a savings-bank deposit will at least retain the value of its principal.

At this point it is perhaps necessary to define our terms. By a "moderate" inflation I mean one that brings an average price rise of less than 10 percent a year. By a "double-digit" inflation, I shall mean one, as the adjective implies, that brings an annual price rise of anything between 10 and 99 percent. And by a "hyperinflation" I shall mean one that brings an annual price rise even higher than that.

This division is arbitrary, but it is not my own. It follows roughly what have lately become common newspaper designations. To call any inflationary rise of less than 10 percent a year a "moderate" one would until very recently have astonished any conservative economist. Even an "inflation rate" of as low as 5 percent a year would wipe out half the purchasing power of the dollar every fifteen years, and even an inflation rate of only 2 percent a year would mean an erosion of the purchasing power of the dollar by about one-half in each generation.

The Risks of Holding Common Stocks

Let us return to our inflation-hedging problem. If the investments to get out of are savings-bank deposits and all fixed-return securities, then it would seem to follow that the investments to get into are "equity" securities, or common stocks. But most past results of this have been very disappointing. In the German hyperinflation of 1919–23, it is true, the average price of stocks increased billions of times, but average wholesale prices increased many more billions of times. The net result was that, at the end of the inflation in December 1923, the average price of stocks was equivalent to only one-fourth their gold value in 1913.

The causes of these disappointing results have been somewhat complex. Let us recall once more that in any inflation, individual prices and costs never go up at a uniform rate but at widely different relative rates and times. Cost-price relationships become discoordinated. Individual firms find it increasingly difficult to know or guess what their own future costs or future selling prices are going to be, and what will be the ratio between them. During an inflation demand shifts quickly from one product to another. This makes it increasingly difficult to plan production ahead, or to estimate future profit margins. In the later stages of an inflation, wage rates are more certain to go up than individual prices. Even if aggregate profits increase in monetary terms, the range of deviation and dispersion is much greater as between different firms. The investor faces increasing uncertainty. This always tends to lower stock prices.

Because the future of the business is increasingly uncertain, corporations become more reluctant to pay out dividends. If, as in many cases, profits are particularly high in money terms, if inventories and plant and equipment are constantly rising in price, more and more plant managers conclude that the best use of their current profits is to plow them back immediately into expansion of the business. This seems especially the most profitable thing to do in a hyperinflation. It then seems foolish to declare dividends when, by the time the stockholders receive them, they may be worth much less than they were when declared.

146

But all this tends to have a demoralizing effect on the stock-holders. They cannot afford to hold many investments that yield them little or nothing. They need current income to live on, and more and more of it in monetary terms. No matter how much the theoretical book value of the shares, few can afford to buy or to hold them.

Gold

The next inflation hedge we have to consider is the purchase of gold. This seems to many the best hedge of all. They remember that in the great German inflation those Germans who consistently bought gold whenever and to the extent they could, and held it until the inflation ended, came out with at least their principal intact. From a strictly economic point of view, buying gold in a major inflation and holding it probably presents the least risk of capital loss of any investment or speculation.

But it also has serious drawbacks. Hoarded gold yields no interest. Either the holder must have some other source of current income to meet his day-to-day living expenses in the depreciating paper currency, or he must sell a certain amount of his gold every week out of his hoard. Otherwise he must sit with his gold till the end of his life or until the inflation is over, whichever comes first.

(And how can he know when the inflation is "over"? If he were a Frenchman he should have bought gold in early July 1914. But now, sixty-four years later, inflation in France is still going on. Technically, of course, it is not the same inflation: there have been any number of "stabilizations" and "currency reforms" in between. Catching every stabilization and every resumption of inflation would not have been easy.)

In addition to not yielding any income return, holding gold is subject to heavy *political* risks. For a whole generation the U.S. government made private possession of gold illegal. When it was once more permitted, Treasury authorities seemed for a while to take a malicious satisfaction in dumping gold on the international market to depress its price. This was called part of the process of "phasing gold out of the monetary system."

There is no reason to think that the political animus against "gold hoarders" and "goldbugs" is permanently over. The possibility of a discriminatory capital-gains tax on gold "profits," or even of outright confiscation, cannot be wholly dismissed. We must remember that in 1933, when private citizens began to exercize their clear legal right to convert their Federal Reserve notes and gold certificates into gold, President Franklin D. Roosevelt suspended the conversion, ordered the citizens to exchange their gold for paper money, and made it illegal for private citizens to hold or own gold. In other words, the government not only broke its solemn and explicit pledge to convert its notes into gold on demand, but treated the holder (and dupe) who had taken the pledge seriously as the real culprit. And the Supreme Court later upheld the president's act and the new law.

Trading in Commodities

Let us turn now to the advisability of speculating in other precious metals, such as silver and platinum, and, still more broadly, in any of the commodities that are traded on the great speculative exchanges: copper, cattle, cotton, lumber, coffee, cocoa, sugar, hogs, pork bellies, wheat, corn, oats, soybeans, and so on.

Trading in silver has some of the advantages of trading in gold, but also shares some of the political risks. In nearly all the other commodities, however, we are getting into an area better left to the professional speculator. It is not only necessary for the trader to know a great deal about the special supply-and-demand situation of the particular commodity he is trading in, but he has to take into account all the costs and risks of trading in and out—the costs and risks of buying on margin, paying interest on borrowed money, paying commissions, and losing because of the constant gap between bid and asked prices. For even if the general trend of the market for the commodity he trades in is upward, there are sure to be violent price fluctuations both ways; and he may find himself being "whipsawed."

Finally, he must take into account the heavy toll of the capital-gains tax. We will return to this last problem later.

We come now to a miscellaneous group of objects frequently resorted to as inflation hedges. One of these is diamonds. These, like gold, have the advantage of a negligible storage charge. But the "investor" in these will need expert advice and appraisal, which involve a cost, and if he is not in the business he must either buy at the retail price and sell at the wholesale, or pay high commissions. In addition, he must keep in mind that his diamonds, being each in some degree unique, will not be as "liquid," or as readily salable, as gold, stocks, or commodities on the exchanges.

Similar and even more emphatic warnings must be given about the speculative buying of paintings and other art objects. The layman reads of huge profits made by the early acquisition and later sale of, say, the French Impressionists, and fancies he can duplicate the achievement. But fortunes can be lost as well as made in paintings. The trick for the person who wants to speculate in them is either to have impeccable taste or a shrewd market sense of the next swing of an art fashion or vogue and of how long it will last. Failing this, he needs expert advice—which may also go wrong. Again, whoever is not himself in the business must pay a substantial dealer's commission when he wants to buy and face the problem of finding a buyer to unload on when he wants to sell.

This leads us to the question of the advisability of buying tangible luxuries of all kinds—antique or expensive modern furniture, vases and similar art objects, personal jewelry, a new car, a yacht, a private plane—anything to get out of depreciating cash and into "real goods."

This is what nearly everybody tries to do when he becomes aware that he is in a hyperinflation. It is hard to offer any general advice about it; too much depends on the advisability of each purchase. It is often a final act of desperation rather than a shrewd provision for the future. One of its ironic consequences is that some economists point to this desperation-buying as a sign of an "expanding economy."

Real Estate

I have left to nearly last the discussion of a very important hedge: the acquisition of real estate. The problem is not a simple one. We must consider at least four different options: (1) the purchase of a home, or perhaps of a bigger and more expensive home, (2) the purchase of raw land, (3) the purchase of residential property—apartments or detached houses—for the purpose of renting, and (4) the purchase of commercial property for one's own business or for rental.

Each of these choices involves its own risks and its own comparative advantages and disadvantages. The advantage of purchasing one's own home or a much better home during an inflationary period is the most obvious. You do not get an immediate monetary return, but you do get an immediate return in added enjoyment. And you have the satisfaction of knowing, if you have bought wisely, that the monetary value of your property is rising as long as the inflation lasts. Even if you buy or build late in an inflation, and pay a much higher price than you would have had to pay a year or ten years previously, you can still expect a further rise in the monetary value of your investment. You may have to pay a high interest rate for a mortgage, but you may more than compensate by paying it off in depreciating dollars. Your main real problems will be a rising cost of maintenance, repairs, and taxes. True, the neighborhood you have chosen may deteriorate, but it may also improve.

With the speculative purchase of raw land, you face a quite different problem. You seldom have to worry about upkeep, and not at all about repairs. Raw land has the advantage that its selling price tends to capitalize not only past and existing inflation, but the average expectations about future inflation. On the other hand, the owner usually gets no enjoyment or other use value out of raw land, and it yields him no monetary return. Instead, he is out of pocket year by year for taxes, which tend to increase with the inflation. And land is illiquid; he cannot sell a particular parcel easily and quickly. In the German hyperinflation of 1919–23 there were men sitting with large tracts of land of high nominal monetary value, but lacking the cash to meet their current living expenses.

The purchase of residential property for rental will normally yield a net income over taxes and maintenance charges, but the owner often faces the danger of a sudden imposition of rent control. The more severe the inflation becomes. the more likely rent controls become. The owner can be trapped in compulsory losses.

The purchase of commercial property tends to avoid the danger of rent control, but it also involves greater risks in finding and keeping a tenant. If the owner puts up an office building or a factory on speculation, he may find that he has built the wrong size or kind of office building or factory.

150

Foreign Investments

I have left till last a form of inflation hedge that might logically have been mentioned much earlier. But I have postponed its discussion because, until the later and worst stages of an inflation, it is a form of hedge usually resorted to only by a comparatively small and sophisticated group of bankers and businessmen. This is the acquisition of foreign currencies and investment in foreign securities, businesses or property. It should be obvious that this is a form of hedge that should be undertaken only by somebody who knows what he is doing, who has an intimate knowledge of the foreign country in which he is investing, or who knows where to get expert and disinterested advice. Many foreigners in the past have invested in dollars and in American securities; it is a little awkward for Americans now to be trying to do the reverse.

The risks of this type of hedge are great. It is extremely difficult to "watch" one's foreign investments. No foreign country is today on a gold basis, or exempt from a possible spurt of internal inflation. When a small country, like Switzerland, begins to find itself such an "inflation-refuge" country, it becomes embarrassed by excessive refuge deposits and tries to discourage or penalize them. And Americans who try to invest their capital abroad are also liable to find themselves increasingly discouraged by domestic legislation. There are apt to be laws and penalties against capital outflow. No matter how discriminatory or unfair these are, they are likely to win popular approval. The assumption will be that only the rich and unpatriotic are able or likely to resort to such a "flight of capital."

Our review of possible inflation hedges has not been on the whole encouraging. We have seen that each attempted hedge has its particular attractions, risks, and shortcomings. Our survey of the major possibilities may also lead us to suspect that there is no one single type of hedge or purchase to be at all times preferred to any of the others. On the contrary, your success will depend much less on what you buy than on when you buy it, at what price, how long you hold it, and at what price you sell it.

No one thing, in an inflation, goes up steadily and dependably and faster than everything else. In a major inflation, even a com-

151

modity that makes a spectacular long-run advance often takes sudden downward plunges in the midst of that advance. Ruinous losses have been suffered by some speculators in gold who were unable to hold on.

At any one time—for a week or a month, say—one commodity will be going up faster than any other. But it is in the nature of speculative markets that the particular front-runner will be constantly changing. An omniscient speculator, foreseeing what the next front-runner was going to be, would sell even a rising commodity to buy this faster-rising one. He would know just when to buy and when to sell each particular thing, and would be constantly changing his "investment."

But not only is no one omniscient; no one is smart enough, or consistently lucky enough, to afford to act this way. The cumulative risks and costs would be prohibitive. First of all would be the cost in study and time. A speculator of the type described would have to devote his full day to his speculation; he could not engage in any other business or profession. He would suffer the repeated costs of getting in and out of his incessant swaps—from the inevitable gap between the bid and asked prices, and from the constant commissions.

Capital-Gains Taxes

And under present laws any successful inflation-hedger would pay ruinous capital-gains taxes. He would pay a capital-gains tax even on nonexistent capital gains, which would happen whenever his monetary gain, for example, was smaller in percentage than that of the average rise in prices in the period. And present laws would allow him, on the average, only a grossly inadequate offset for real losses. The average federal capital-gains tax comes to 25 percent, and the state capital-gains tax—in New York, for example—comes to another 5 percent. It has been frequently pointed out that, even when the "take" of a gambling casino averages only 2 or 3 percent, those who gamble long enough against it must all eventually lose. What must be the result when the take of the "house" is 30 percent?

It should be obvious that the whole present American tax system not only discourages effort and enterprise, but makes it all but impossible for a law-abiding citizen to protect himself against the ravages of the inflation that the government's own policies impose upon him.

A period of inflation is almost inevitably also a period when demagogy and an antibusiness mentality are rampant. If implacable enemies of the country had deliberately set out to undermine and destroy the incentives of the middle classes to work and save, they could hardly have contrived a more effective set of weapons than the present combination of inflation, subsidies, handouts, and confiscatory taxes that our own politicians have imposed upon us.

Tipsters, advertising their services, often lead the unsuspecting citizen to believe that inflation offers him exceptional opportunities to make a fortune. So far as the overwhelming majority of us are concerned, this is exactly the opposite of what it does. In addition to all the special factors we have just been discussing, there are two overriding considerations. One is that, in hedging against inflation, each of us can protect himself only at the expense of someone else. Every time we buy some commodity as a hedge, we tend to raise the price for the next buyer. It is possible successfully to practice inflation hedging individually, but never generally.

At best, inflation can benefit one group only at the expense of other groups. The price of what you have to sell can go up more or faster than the average price of what you have to buy only if the price of what *other* people have to sell to you goes up less or slower than the price of what they have to buy from you. The net amount of any real gain from inflation must be offset by at least an equivalent amount of real loss. The political appeal of inflation comes from fostering the illusion in the great majority of voters that they will somehow get the better of the swindle, and profit at the expense of a few unidentified victims.

But the overall situation should be clear. Inflation is a form of tax, a tax that we all collectively must pay. If the government spends, say, $70 billion more in a given year than it imposes in taxes, and pays out the difference by issuing $70 billion more in paper money, all those of us who are not paid part of that deficit money from the government must collectively forego the equivalent of $70 billion in goods, services, or savings.

For every outstanding profiteer from a major and prolonged

153

inflation there are crowds of losers. Those who spread the false belief that the individual, by a few simple hedges open to all, can easily save himself from inflation, or that one is even presented with a special opportunity to make a fortune from it, reduce the opposition to it and encourage its continuance. There is no safe hedge against inflation except to stop it.

22

Why Inflation Is Worldwide

For the first time in the history of the world, practically every country is on a paper-money basis and every country is inflating. It is instructive to recall how this has come about.

For a full explanation, we must go back at least sixty-four years to the outbreak of World War I in 1914. The first thing that happened, almost on the day the war broke out, was that the belligerents suspended the convertibility of their currencies into gold.

It is important to remember why they did this. They did not do it because they suddenly discovered that gold was out of date, that it was a "barbarous relic," that a paper standard was altogether more modern, efficient, and scientific. They did it, on the contrary, because gold had suddenly become too valuable. It was a precious war resource. The belligerent governments knew they would need it to buy arms and food from neutrals abroad, and that gold was the only currency other countries would accept. They found this out very quickly. England, for example, declared war on Germany on August 4. A run developed on the Bank of England. The gold reserve, which had been valued at 38.6 million pounds sterling in July, was pulled down within a few days to 26 million pounds. Convertibility was suspended on August 5. In addition, export controls were imposed on gold.

155

When the First World War ended, some of the belligerents went back to the gold standard. England again is the outstanding example of the problems of doing this and of the mistakes that were made. Resumption of gold payments was undertaken at the prewar rate for the pound in 1925. But two greatly changed circumstances were overlooked. First, there had been an enormous expansion meanwhile in the issuance of British currency and credit, that is, in the amount of paper promises that people might want to convert into gold. And second, as a result of that, prices had risen substantially. If in 1925 the currency had been made convertible only at a correspondingly higher "price" for gold, the resumption of gold payments might have worked. But the resumption at the old rate made gold too much of a bargain, and forced a contraction of British credit and a fall in prices.

In September 1931, England went off the gold standard once again. The U.S. likewise abandoned the gold standard, at its old rate of $20.67 an ounce, in 1933. Unfortunately, it was not the war and postwar inflations in both countries that were blamed for this result, or the ill-advised retention of the old gold-conversion rates, but the gold standard itself.

When the Second World War broke out in September 1939, many of the world's currencies were again thrown into chaos, and for substantially the same reasons as in World War I. But this time, in July 1944, before the war had even ended, the representatives of some forty-three nations were invited by the United States to a conference at Bretton Woods, New Hampshire, to try to set up a new international currency system.

What they set up, under the leadership of Lord Keynes of England and Harry Dexter White of the United States, was a compromise designed to please the advocates of paper money, "flexibility," and "national independence," or "self-determination," of currencies, but at the same time to reassure conservatives that these currencies would retain a "link" to gold. The supposed great merit of the new system was that the monetary role of gold—the "tyranny" of gold—would be drastically reduced.

Only one currency, the U.S. dollar, would have to be convertible into gold—and even then no longer at the demand of anybody who held dollars, but only at the request of foreign central banks. All the other currencies were to be kept convertible merely into the dollar. With the dollar anchored to gold, and all the other currencies tied to the dollar, stability was to be assured, and the need for gold reserves to be minimized.

The system seemed to relieve every other country but the United States from strict monetary discipline. If any country got into trouble, it was assured almost automatic loans and credit to bail it out. The agreement also provided that any nation could at any time devalue its currency by up to 10 percent, and explicity stipulated that "the Fund shall raise no objection." The real but unstated and unacknowledged purpose of the Bretton Woods Agreements, as the present writer pointed out at the time (in *The American Scholar,* Winter 1944–45) was "to make resort to inflation easy, smooth, and above all respectable."

As early as 1949 the system started to break down. The British pound was devalued 30 percent on September 18 of that year—from $4.03 to $2.80. Twenty-five other currencies were devalued within the following week. In succeeding years there were literally hundreds of devaluations of currencies in the International Monetary Fund.

Responsibility on the U.S.

What had been overlooked from the beginning was the enormous increase in the burden and responsibility that the Bretton Woods arrangements put upon the United States. Other countries could hold dollar reserves on the assumption that this was just as good as holding gold. But their currency stability was, in fact, made dependent on the soundness of the dollar.

Yet successive U.S. governments remained completely oblivious of the gravity of the responsibility they had assumed. Our officials kept undermining the dollar through foreign aid, huge domestic spending, chronic and mounting budget deficits, and by pushing down domestic interest rates and increasing the money supply. By 1968 we had practically ceased keeping the dollar convertible into gold, even for central banks. And on August 15, 1971, we abandoned the gold standard openly and officially.

Our repudiation of our solemn commitment was followed by mounting inflation, devaluations, and monetary demoralization everywhere. There seemed no longer any point in maintaining fixed exchange rates. There was not even any agreement on what they could be fixed to.

The three tables that follow were published over a twenty-year period by Citibank (formerly First National City Bank of New York) in its *Monthly Economic Letter*. They appear here with the bank's permission.

Table 1 appeared in the bank's letter of December 1956. It shows the depreciation of the purchasing power of money in each of sixteen countries listed, in the ten years from 1946 to 1956, as measured by the rise in official cost of living figures. The third column gives the annual rate of depreciation in those years, compounded.

Table 1

Country	Indexes of Value of Money[a]		Annual Rates of Depreciation (compounded)
	1946	1956[b]	1946–56
Switzerland	100	86	1.5%
Germany	100	72	3.2
India	100	72	3.2
United States	100	71	3.4
Venezuela	100	70	3.5
Netherlands	100	67	4.9
Canada	100	65	4.2
South Africa	100	65	4.2
Sweden	100	65	4.3
United Kingdom	100[c]	65	4.6
New Zealand	100	59	5.2
France	100[d]	58	6.5
Mexico	100	47	7.4
Australia	100	46	7.5
Brazil	100	26	12.7
Chile	100	5	25.3

Note: Depreciation computed from unrounded data.

[a] Measured by rise in official cost of living or consumer price indexes.

[b] Latest month available.

[c] 1947.

[d] 1948.

The bank's original purpose in making this calculation was to show how much annual interest a saver in each country would have had to receive, and reinvest at compounded interest, to have the same amount of purchasing power in 1956 as he had in 1946. In nearly every country, the table revealed, if he had bought and held his own government's bonds, he would not only have received no net interest, but would have lost heavily on his real principal.

Table 2 (pp. 160–61), published in the bank's monthly letter of July 1967, shows the depreciation of the purchasing power of the money of forty-five countries. It carries the record from 1956 to 1966. In addition, it calculates the annual rate of currency depreciation in each of these countries during the ten years 1956 to 1966.

Table 3 (pp. 162–63), which appeared in the September 1976 letter, compares the purchasing power of money for fifty countries—twenty-five industrial countries and others in Europe, and twenty-five "less developed" countries—from 1965 to 1975. It also calculates their annual rate of depreciation for the five years 1965 to 1970, and for the five years 1970 to 1975.

From these tables the interested reader can calculate the approximate depreciation over the full thirty-year period of any one of at least sixteen of these currencies, and the twenty-year depreciation of most of the rest. I had originally intended to consolidate these three tables into a single one, but it seems to me more instructive to present them separately in their original form, because much more is brought out by comparisons between them, and consolidated tables would add little of importance.

What the three tables show is not only that for nearly all these countries the inflation is at least thirty years old, but that its long-term tendency has been to accelerate rather than diminish. In the ten years from 1946 to 1956, the median depreciation among the sixteen currencies included in the table was 4.3 percent a year. In the next ten years—1956 to 1966—the median depreciation among the forty-five currencies included was still only 3.4 percent per year. In the five years from 1965 to 1970, however, the median annual depreciation among the currencies of twenty-five industrial countries was back to 4.4 percent and of twenty-five less developed countries to 4.2 percent. And in the five years from 1970 to 1975 the median annual depreciation among the industrial countries had risen to 8.5 percent, and among the less developed countries to 10.3 percent.

I have compared the *median* rates of currency depreciation in

Table 2

Country	Indexes of Value of Money		Annual Rates of Depreciation (compounded)
	1956	**1966**	**1956–66**
Guatemala	100	100	0.0%
Venezuela	100	90	1.1
Honduras	100	86	1.5
United States	100	84	1.8
Luxembourg	100	83	1.9
Canada	100	82	2.0
Australia	100	82	2.0
Greece	100	81	2.1
Thailand	100	80	2.2
Belgium	100	80	2.2
South Africa	100	80	2.2
West Germany	100	79	2.3
Portugal	100	78	2.4
Switzerland	100	78	2.4
New Zealand	100	77	2.6
Ecuador	100	76	2.6
Austria	100	75	2.8
U.A.R. (Egypt)	100	75	2.9
United Kingdom	100	74	2.9
Italy	100	72	3.2
Ireland	100	72	3.2
Norway	100	72	3.3
Netherlands	100	71	3.4
Pakistan	100	70	3.5
Iran	100	70	3.5
Philippines	100	70	3.6
Denmark	100	69	3.6
Mexico	100	69	3.7
Sweden	100	68	3.8
Japan	100	66	4.0
France	100	62	4.7
Finland	100	60	4.9
China (Taiwan)	100	58	5.2

Table 2

Country	Indexes of Value of Money		Annual Rates of Depreciation (compounded)
	1956	1966	1956–66
Israel	100	58	5.4%
India	100	57	5.5
Spain	100	49	6.9
Vietnam	100	46	7.4
Turkey	100	45	7.7
Peru	100	41	8.5
Korea	100	33	10.5
Colombia	100	32	10.8
Bolivia	100	25	13.0
Chile	100	10	20.6
Argentina	100	6	24.5
Brazil	100	2	31.0

Note: Depreciation computed from unrounded data. Value of money is measured by reciprocals of offical cost of living or consumer price indexes.

these four periods—that is, the annual rate of depreciation in the middle country in each table—because to have figured and presented the *average* annual rate of depreciation shown in the respective tables would have given a much exaggerated impression of the extent of the general worldwide inflation. To cite only the median depreciation, on the other hand, greatly understates what has happened. In the first decade listed—1946 to 1956—for example, the Chilean peso lost 95 percent of its value. In the second decade—1956 to 1966—the Brazilian cruzeiro lost 98 percent even of its 1956 value, though it had already lost 74 percent of its 1946 value in the preceding decade. Then in the decade from 1965 to 1975 the Chilean and Argentine pesos lost more than 99 percent even of their appallingly shrunken 1965 purchasing powers. Few of us can adequately conceive the extent of the tragedies that these depreciations brought to millions of families in the countries involved.

Table 3

Industrialized Countries and Other Europe

	Indexes of value of money (1965=100)		Annual rate of depreciation of money	
	1970	**1975**	**'65-'70**	**'70-'75**
Switzerland	85	58	3.3%	7.1%
West Germany	88	65	2.8	5.8
United States	81	59	4.1	6.3
Denmark	73	47	6.2	8.5
Austria	85	60	3.2	6.8
Canada	83	58	3.7	6.8
Netherlands	79	52	4.6	7.9
France	81	53	4.2	8.1
Japan	77	45	5.2	10.2
Norway	79	53	4.7	7.7
Belgium	84	56	3.4	7.7
Luxembourg	86	61	3.0	6.7
Sweden	80	55	4.4	7.3
South Africa	85	55	3.2	8.5
Australia	86	53	3.0	9.3
Greece	88	49	2.4	11.0
Yugoslavia	59	24	10.0	16.1
Italy	86	50	2.9	10.2
Spain	78	44	4.8	10.8
Finland	64	37	8.5	10.4
Ireland	77	41	5.0	11.7
Turkey	67	29	7.6	15.7
New Zealand	79	48	4.7	9.3
Britain	80	43	4.4	11.5
Portugal	74	36	6.0	13.1
Median rates	—	—	4.4	8.5

Table 3

Less-Developed Countries

	Indexes of value of money (1965=100)		Annual rate of depreciation of money	
	1970	1975	'65-'70[a]	'70-'75[a]
India	72	42	6.4%	10.4%
Singapore	94	57	1.2	9.1
Panama	92	65	1.6	6.7
Malaysia	94	66	1.3	6.8
China (Taiwan)	81	45	4.2	10.9
Philippines	75	37	5.6	13.2
Honduras	92	68	1.7	5.9
Iran	93	59	1.4	8.6
Thailand	88	58	2.5	8.0
Bolivia	75	32	5.6	15.8
Venezuela	92	70	1.6	5.4
Paraguay	94	54	1.3	10.3
Ecuador	79	42	4.5	10.2
Jamaica	77	39	5.0	12.9
Trinidad/Tobago	83	45	3.7	11.6
Colombia	62	26	9.2	16.0
Mexico	84	47	3.5	10.8
Kenya	91	54	1.8	9.9
S. Korea	58	29	10.2	13.1
Israel	82	32	3.9	17.3
Peru	63	35	8.9	11.2
Brazil	30	11	21.5	17.4
Zaire	36	15	18.5	15.7
Chile	31	b	20.9	67.5
Argentina	41	b	16.2	39.2
Median rates	—	—	4.2	10.3

[a] Compounded monthly.

[b] Less than 1.

163

No Fixed Standard Left

In one regard, the generally increased worldwide rate of inflation since 1970 was what might have been expected. For when the United States adandoned convertibility of the dollar into gold, it not only set an example in itself demoralizing, but it left no fixed standard for other currencies to hook themselves onto.

(The Special Drawing Rights—SDRs—issued by the International Monetary Fund had never been directly convertible into gold, and they were quickly revalued as a daily-fluctuating average, or "market basket," of sixteen paper currencies, each itself changing hourly.)

But the American desertion of gold convertibility in 1971 was, of course, merely an additional cause of a worldwide inflation that had been going on ever since the outbreak of World War II. That inflation started when the governments directly involved had to increase their budget expenditures at almost any cost in order to prosecute the war. But when the war was over, they did not prudently return to their previous level of expenditures. They had also enormously increased their tax revenues, even if not proportionately to their war expenditures, and instead of cutting taxes back to peacetime levels, they increased or added all sorts of "welfare" measures—mainly vote-buying handouts to pressure groups—to make use of the new revenues. What no one sufficiently realized was that once these welfare measures were established, it would come to be regarded as political suicide by the politicians in power to attempt to cut them off or even diminish them.

There has been still a third reason for the increasingly widespread inflation in recent years. The Bretton Woods Agreements, as we have seen, gave explicit sanction to devaluation, provided it did not exceed 10 percent in any single step. Now when "Alphasia," which borders on and does a lot of trade with "Betavia," devalues, a first effect is for the citizens of Alphasia to increase their exports to Betavia, and to reduce their imports from it, because immediately following the devaluation the cost of Alphasia's goods are lower in Betavia and the cost of Betavia's goods are higher in Alphasia. But this means that Alphasia's devaluation can seriously unbalance and disrupt Betavia's trade. This may lead Betavia to declare a "protective" devaluation.

The only thing that seems likely to diminish such competitive devaluation, if not to bring it to a halt, is an increasing recognition within each country that the supposed trade advantages of a devaluation are both transitory and illusory, and that the great body of the citizens of the country that either initiates or follows the practice are in the long run hurt far more than helped by it.

But on top of all these there has been still a fourth major reason for worldwide inflation. This is the fixed idea that inflation is necessary to prevent or reduce unemployment. To the extent that there is any truth in this, it is true only for one reason: As long as the special legal immunities and privileges now granted to labor unions in most countries enable those unions to exact wage rates higher than the existing market can sustain, more inflation (causing higher prices) will seem necessary to make the higher wage rates payable. Otherwise, as we have seen, the belief in the necessity for inflation as a remedy for unemployment has no real basis.

Lord Keynes gets perhaps too much credit—or blame—as the inventor of this myth. When his *General Theory of Employment, Interest, and Money* appeared in 1936, our own government, for one, had already been following policies of uninterrupted deficit spending for six fiscal years. Keynes's theories simply supplied a more elaborate rationale to justify what politicians had already been doing. But his authority and prestige prolonged and intensified the disease.

23

The Search for an Ideal Money

For more than a century economists have toyed with the idea of designing or inventing an ideal money. So far no two of them seem to have precisely agreed on the detailed nature of such a money. But they do seem, at the moment, to agree on at least one negative point. There is probably no economist today who would defend the international and American monetary systems just as they are. No one openly defends the violent daily and hourly fluctuations in exchange rates, the steadily increasing unpredictability of future import, export, or domestic prices. Every newspaper reader fears that commodity prices will be higher next year and still higher the year after that. Even the man in the street, in brief, senses that the world is drifting toward monetary chaos.

But concerning the remedy we find little agreement. Inflation is bad, some agree. Yes, but it isn't as bad as depression and unemployment, and at least it puts off those greater evils, so we must have just a little more inflation as long as these evils threaten us. Inflation is bad, others agree, but it has nothing to do with the monetary system. Rising prices are brought about by the greed and rapacity of sellers; they could promptly be stopped by price controls. Or, inflation is bad, still others concede; and it is brought about by the increase in the quantity of money and credit. But this is not the fault of the monetary system itself, but of the blunders and misdeeds of the politicians or the bureaucrats in charge of it.

Even those who admit that there is something wrong with the monetary system itself cannot agree on the reforms needed in that system. Scores of such reforms have been proposed.

The reformers, however, tend to fall into two main groups. One of these would have nothing to do with a gold, a silver, or any other commodity standard, but would leave the issuance and control of the currency entirely in the hands of the State. The other group would return to some form of the gold standard.

Each of these two groups may again be divided into two schools. In what I shall call the statist, or paper-money, group, one school would leave everything to the day-to-day discretion of government monetary authorities, and the other would subject these authorities to strict quantitative controls. And in the gold group, likewise, one school would allow discretion, within vague but wide limits, to private bankers and government authorities, while the second would impose severe and definite limits on that discretion.

So we have, then, four main schools of monetary theorists. Nearly every currency proposal can be classified under one of them.

Paper Money without Control

Let us begin with the paper-money statists, who would leave the power of controlling the nature, quantity, and value of our money solely in the hands of the politicians in office or the bureaucrats they appoint. This is the worst imaginable monetary system, but it is the one that prevails nearly everywhere in the world today. It has brought about practically universal inflation, unprecedented uncertainty, and economic disruption.

None of this is accidental. It was built into the system deliberately adopted at a conference of forty-four nations at Bretton Woods in 1944, under the guidance of Harry Dexter White of the U.S. and Lord Keynes of Great Britain. The ostensible purpose of that conference was to increase "international cooperation" and, believe it or not, to "stabilize" currencies and exchange rates.

The chief architects sincerely believed (though they did not as openly avow) that this end could best be achieved by phasing gold out of the monetary system. So they put the world, in effect, not on a gold but on a dollar standard. The value of every other currency was to be maintained by making it convertible into the American dollar at a fixed official exchange rate.

The system still had one tie to gold. The dollar itself was to be kept convertible into that metal at $35 an ounce. But this tie was weakened in two ways. Other countries could keep their currencies stabilized in terms of the dollar, not through the operations of a free foreign exchange market (as under the pre–World War I gold standard) but by government sales or purchases of dollars—in other words, by government pegging operations. And dollars were no longer convertible into gold on demand by anybody who held them; they were convertible only by foreign central banks. The United States could even (off the record) use its great political and economic power—which in time it did—to indicate to any central bank with the effrontery to ask for gold that this was not considered a friendly act.

So the artificial stability that the Bretton Woods system was able to maintain for a few years was not the result of any real attempt by each country to keep its own currency sound—by refraining from excessive issuance of money and credit—but of government pegging operations and gentlemen's agreements not to upset the apple cart.

This arrangement proved, in the end, unwise, unsound, and unstable. The system was able to maintain the appearance of stability only by the stronger currencies constantly rushing to the rescue of the weaker. The U.S., say, would rush in and lend Britain millions of dollars. Or the U.S. Treasury would buy millions of pounds. It would do the like for other currencies in crisis. But using the stronger currencies to support the weaker only weakened the stronger currencies. When the United States Treasury bought millions of pounds with dollars, it in effect got these dollars by printing them.

And so when the dollar itself, as the result of our own recklessness, began to turn bad, and when we went off the gold standard openly in August 1971, other nations were affected. Germany, for instance, under the terms of the Bretton Woods agreements, had to buy billions of dollars to keep the mark from going above its official parity. And where did Germany get the billions of marks necessary to buy the billions of dollars? By printing them.

So the faster-inflating nations almost systematically exported their inflations to the slower-inflating nations. And this almost systematically brought the world toward its present inflationary chaos.

True, the nations with stronger currencies, even when they felt obliged by their Bretton Woods agreement to buy weaker currencies, did not *have* to increase their own money supply to buy them. Neither Germany nor any other nation that acquired dollars *had* to use the dollars as added central bank "reserves" against which they could issue still more of their own currency. They could have "sterilized" their reserves of dollars. Or they could have reduced their other government expenditures correspondingly when they felt obliged to buy dollars, or raised the amount by added taxation, instead of simply printing more marks or whatever. But these would have been very difficult decisions. They might have endangered the tenure of the governments that made them. What they chose seemed under the circumstances the path of least resistance.

What has to be made crystal clear, if we are to lay the foundations for any permanent sound monetary reform, is that the present worldwide inflationary chaos is not a mere accident. It is not something that has happened in spite of the wonderfully modern and enlightened International Monetary Fund system. It is something that has happened precisely *because* of that system. It is, in fact, its almost inevitable result.

It was precisely the kind of "international cooperation" it set up that led to its final breakdown. The countries whose policies were chronically leading them into currency crises should have been obliged to pay the penalty. The faltering currencies should not have been rescued by the central banks of other countries. It was exactly because the soft-currency countries knew that an American or international safety net would be almost automatically spread out to save them that they chronically got themselves into more trouble.

As it was, the system kept breaking down anyway, but there was a sort of open conspiracy to ignore its fundamental unsoundness. In September 1949, the British pound was devalued by 30 percent, from $4.03 to $2.80. When this happened some twenty-five other countries devalued within a single week. In November 1967, the British pound was devalued once more, this time from $2.80 to $2.40. There have been in fact hundreds of devaluations of currencies in the International Monetary Fund since it opened for business in 1946. In its *Monthly Bulletin* the Fund has printed literally millions of statistics a year, but it has steadfastly refused, up to now, to publish one figure—the total number of these devaluations.

Paper Money Under "Strict" Controls

Enough of this. It should be no longer necessary to prove how bad the Bretton Woods system turned out to be. Few people, aside from the bureaucrats whose jobs are at stake, would seriously try to glue it together again. The system is dead. Unfortunately the corpse has not been buried.

Let us turn to the next candidate, the proposals of the so-called Monetarists. Two things may be said in favor of the Monetarists. First, they do recognize the close connection between the quantity of money and the purchasing-power of the monetary unit. And second, they do acknowledge the importance of imposing strict and explicit limits on the issuance of money. But there are serious weaknesses both in their factual assumptions and in their policy proposals.

It is true that there is a close relation between the outstanding supply of money and the buying power of the individual monetary unit. But it is not true that this relation is inversely proportional or in any other way fixed and dependable. Nor is it true that there is any fixed "lag" between an increase of a given percentage in the "growth" of the money supply and an increase of the same percentage in prices. The statistics on which this conclusion is based are at best inadequate. They do not cover enough currencies over long enough periods.

What happens during a typical inflation is that in its early stages commodity prices do not rise as fast as the supply of money is increased, and in its later stages prices rise much faster than the supply of money is increased.

Monetarists will dismiss this whole comparison as unfair and irrelevant. They do not regard themselves as proposing inflation at all. To them inflation is *defined* not as an increase in the money supply, but only as a rise in prices. And their proposal, as they see it, is to increase the stock of money 3 to 5 percent a year *just to keep the price "level" from falling*. They propose an annual increase

170

in the money stock merely to compensate for an expected annual increase of 3 percent or more in the "productivity" of the economy.

The Monetarists' proposal rests on a false factual assumption. There is no automatic and dependable annual increase in productivity of 3 percent or any other fixed rate. The increase in productivity that has occurred in the United States in recent years is the result of saving, investment, and technical progress. None of these is automatic. In fact, in the last few years, the usual productivity measures have actually been declining.

Wholly apart from the formidable mathematical and statistical problems involved, which space does not permit me to go into, the maintenance of the price level is a dubious goal. It is based on the assumption that falling prices are somehow deflationary, and that in any case they tend to bring about recession. This assumption is questionable. When the stock of money is not increased, falling prices are a normal result of increased production and economic progress. They need not bring recession, because the falling prices are themselves the result of falling production costs. Real profit margins are not reduced. Money wage-rates may not increase, but real wages will increase because the same money will buy more. Falling prices with continued or rising prosperity have occurred frequently in our history.

In our present world of powerful and aggressive labor unions, with legally built-in coercive powers, the Monetarists do have a legitimate fear that such unions will not be satisfied with increased purchasing power for the same money wages. In that case, when such unions ask and get excessive wage rates, they may bring on unemployment and recession. But this danger will exist under any monetary system whatever, as long as the government and the politicians in power retain their present one-sided labor laws and union ideology.

The central and fatal flaw of the Monetarist proposal is its extreme political naivete. It puts the power of controlling the quantity, the quality, and the purchasing power of our money entirely in the hands of the State, that is, of the politicians and bureaucrats in office.

I am tempted to add that it leaves this power entirely to the *discretion,* the arbitrary caprice, of the temporary holders of office in the State. The Monetarists would deny this. They would limit the discretion of the monetary managers, they contend, by a strict rule. The managers would be ordered to increase the stock of money by only 2, or 3, or 4, or 5 percent per year; and this figure would be written into the law, or into the Constitution.

It is a sign of the Monetarists' own vacillation that they have never quite decided whether this figure should be a month-to-month bureaucratic goal, or embodied in a law, or nailed into the Constitution. Nor have they ever definitely decided whether the figure itself should be 2 or 3 or 4 or 5 percent. They can apparently hold their ranks together only by remaining vague.

It is obvious that once the premises of this system were adopted there would be continuous political pressure for inflation. Those who contended that an annual increase of 2 percent in the money stock would be enough would constantly have to combat the fears of their colleagues that this might be too low, threatening to bring on recession. The 3 percenters, again, would have to fight a cease-less rearguard action against the advocates of 4 percent, or these in turn against the champions of 5 percent. And so ad infinitum. Every time a recession seemed imminent, it would be blamed on the lowness of the existing rate of money increase. Agitation would be resumed to boost it.

None of this is a figment of my imagination. It occurs system-atically. On February 20, 1975, Henry Ford II, in presenting a dis-appointing annual report of his motor company, emphasized the need of measures to "assure strong recovery." Among these, he stipulated, "The Federal Reserve must raise the monetary growth rate to the range of 6 to 8 per cent for a short period. As the rate of inflation subsides, real monetary balances increase, and recovery begins, the monetary growth rate should be reduced to prevent a new burst of inflation."

I cite this as only one among scores of examples. It was especially instructive because it came from a businessman and not from a politician.

A month later there was a far more striking illustration. On March 18, 1975, the United States Senate adopted unanimously, 86 to 0, a resolution urging the Federal Reserve Board to expand the money supply in a way "appropriate to facilitating prompt eco-nomic recovery." It also asked the board to consult with the House and Senate banking committes every six months on "objectives and plans" concerning the money supply. This was in effect an order to the Fed to continue inflating, and presumably to increase the rate of inflation. It also put the Fed on notice that whatever it may have previously supposed, it was not independent, but subject to the directions of the politicans in office. The substance of this resolution was later adopted by the full Congress.

The Monetarists' program would inevitably make the monetary system a political football. What else could we expect? Isn't it the height of naivete deliberately to put the power of determining the money supply in the hands of the State, and then expect existing officeholders not to use that power to assure their own tenure of office?

The first requisite of a sound monetary system is that it put the least possible power over the quantity or quality of money in the hands of the politicians.

The Merit of Gold

This brings us to gold. It is the outstanding merit of gold as the monetary standard that it makes the supply and the purchasing power of the monetary unit independent of government, of office holders, of political parties, and of pressure groups. The great merit of gold is precisely that it is scarce; that its quantity is limited by nature; that it is costly to discover, to mine, and to process; and that it cannot be created by political fiat or caprice. It is precisely the merit of the gold standard, finally, that it puts a limit on credit expansion.

But there are two major kinds of gold standard. One is the fractional reserve system, and the other the pure gold, or 100 percent reserve, system.

The fractional-reserve system is the one that developed and prevailed in the Western world in the century from 1815 to 1914. It is what we now call the classical gold standard. It had the so-called advantage of elasticity. And it made possible—we might justly say it was responsible for—the business cycle, the recurrent round of prosperity and recession, of boom and bust.

With the fractional-reserve system what typically happened was that in a given country—let us say Ruritania—borrowers would be given credit by the banks, in the form of demand deposits, and they would launch upon various enterprises. The new money so created, perhaps after taking up a slack in business and employment, would increase Ruritanian prices. Ruritania would become a better place to sell to, and a poorer place to buy from. The balance of trade or payments would begin to turn against it. This would be reflected in a fall in the exchange rate of the Ruritanian currency until the "gold export point" was reached. Gold would then flow out to other countries. In order to stop it, interest rates in Ruritania would have to be raised. With a higher interest rate or a smaller gold base, the volume of currency would be contracted. This would mean a deflation or a crisis followed by a slump.

In brief, the gold standard with a fractional-reserve system tended almost systematically to bring about the cycle of boom and slump.

Under such a system, there is constant political pressure to reduce interest rates or the reserve requirements so that credit expansion—inflation—may be encouraged or continued. It is supposed to be the great advantage of a fractional-reserve system that it allows credit expansion. But what is overlooked is that, no matter how low the required legal reserve is set, there must eventually come a point when the permissible legal credit expansion has been reached. There is then inevitable political pressure to reduce the percentage of required reserves still further.

This has been the history of the system in the United States. The effect—and partly the intention—of the Federal Reserve Act was enormously to increase the potential volume of credit expansion. The required reserves for member banks were reduced by the Federal Reserve Act of 1914 from a range of 15 to 25 percent for the previous national banks to 12 to 18 percent for the new Federal Reserve member banks. In 1917 the required reserves for member banks were reduced still further to a range of 7 to 13 percent.

On top of the inverted pyramid of credit that the member banks were allowed to create, the newly established Federal Reserve banks, which now held the reserves of the member banks, were permitted to erect a still further inverted credit pyramid of their own. The reserve banks were required to carry only a 35 percent reserve against their deposits and a 40 percent gold reserve against their gold notes.

Later the Federal Reserve authorities became more strict in imposing reserve requirements on the member banks (they raised these sharply beginning in 1936, for example). But they continued to be very lenient in setting their own reserve requirements. Between June 1945 and March 1965 the reserve requirements were reduced from 35 and 40 percent to a flat 25 percent. And then they were dropped altogether.

So much for history. What of the future?

If the world, or at least this country, ever returns to its senses, and decides to reestablish a gold standard, the fractional reserve system ought to be abandoned. If by some miracle the U.S. government were to make this decision tomorrow, it could not of course wipe out the already existing supply of fiduciary money and credit, or any substantial part of it, without bringing on a devastating and needless deflation. But the government would at least have to refrain from any further increase in the supply of such fiduciary currency. Assuming that the government were then able to fix upon a workable conversion rate of the dollar into gold, a rate that was sustainable and would not in itself lead to either inflation or deflation, the U.S. could then return to a sound currency and a sound gold basis.

But in the world as it has now become, sunk in hopeless confusion, inflationism, and demagogy, the likelihood of any such development in the foreseeable future is practically nil. The remedy I have suggested rests on the assumption that our government and other governments will become responsible, and suddenly begin doing what is in the long-run interest of the whole body of the citizens, instead of only in the short-run interest—or apparent interest—of special pressure groups. Today this is to expect a miracle.

A Private Money

But the outlook is not hopeless. I began by pointing out that for more than a century individual economists have tried to design an ideal money. Why have they not agreed? Why have their schemes come to nothing? They have failed, I think, because they have practically all begun with the same false assumption—the assumption that the creation and "management" of a monetary system is and ought to be the prerogative of the State.

This has become an almost universal superstition. It is tantamount to agreeing that a monetary system should be made the plaything of the politicians in power.

The proposals of the would-be monetary reformers have failed, in fact, for *two* main reasons. They have failed partly because they have misconceived the primary functions that a monetary system has to serve. Too many monetary reformers have assumed that the chief quality to be desired in a money is to be "neutral." And too many have assumed that this neutrality would be best achieved if they could create a money that would lead to a constant and unchanging "price level."

This was the goal of Irving Fisher in the 1920s, with his "compensated dollar." It is the goal of his present-day disciples, the Monetarists, and their proposal for a government-managed increase in the money supply of 3 to 5 percent a year to keep the price level stable.

I believe, for several reasons, that this goal itself is a questionable one. But what is an even more serious and harmful error on their part is the method by which they propose to achieve this goal. They propose to achieve it by giving the politicians in office the power to manipulate the currency according to some formula concocted by the currency reformers themselves.

What such reformers fail to recognize is that once the politicians and their appointees are granted such powers, they are less likely to use them to pursue the objectives of the reformers than they are to pursue their own objectives. The politicians' own objectives will be those that seem best calculated to keep themselves in power. The particular policy they will assume is most likely to keep them in power is to keep increasing the issuance of money, because this will: (1) increase "purchasing power" and so presumably increase the volume of trade and employment, (2) keep prices going up as fast as union pressure pushes up wages, so that continued employment will be possible, and (3) give subsidies and other handouts to special pressure groups without immediately raising taxes to pay for them. In other words, the best immediate policy for the politicians in power will always appear to them to be inflation.

In sum, the belief that the creation and management of a monetary system ought to be the prerogative of the State—that is, of the politicians in power—is not only false but harmful. For the real solution is just the opposite. *It is to get government, as far as possible, out of the monetary sphere.* And the first step we should insist on is to get our government and the courts not only to permit, but to enforce, voluntary private contracts providing for payment in gold or in terms of gold value.

Let us see what would happen if this were done. As the rate of inflation increased, or became more uncertain, Americans would tend increasingly to make long-term contracts payable in gold. This is because sellers and lenders would become increasingly reluctant to make long-term contracts payable in paper dollars or in irredeemable money-units of any other kind.

This preference for making long-term contracts in gold would apply particularly to international contracts. The buyer or debtor would then either have to keep a certain amount of gold in reserve, or make a forward contract to buy gold, or depend on buying gold in the open spot market with his paper money on the date that his contract fell due. In time, if inflation continued, even current transactions would increasingly be made in gold.

Thus there would grow up, side by side with fiat paper money, a *private* domestic and international gold standard. Each country that permitted this would then be on a dual monetary system, with a daily changing market relation between the two monies. And there would be a private gold system ready to take over completely on the very day that the government's paper money became absolutely worthless—as it did in Germany in November 1923, and in scores of other countries at various times.

Could there be such a private gold standard? To ask such a question is to forget that history and prehistory have already answered it. Private gold coins, and private gold transactions, existed centuries before governments decided to take them over, to nationalize them, so to speak. The argument that the kings and governments put forward for doing this—and it was a plausible one—was that the existing private coins were not of uniform and easily recognizable size, weight, and imprint; that the fineness of their gold content, or whether they were gold at all, could not be easily tested; that the private coins were crude and easily counterfeited; and finally that the legal recourse of the receiver, if he found a coin to be underweight or debased, was uncertain and difficult. But, the king's spokesmen went on to argue, if the coins were uniform, and bore the instantly recognizable stamp of the realm, and if the government itself stood ever ready to prosecute all clippers or counterfeiters, the people could depend on their money. Business transactions would become more efficient and certain, and enormously less time-consuming.

Still another specious argument for a government coinage ap-

177

plied especially to subsidiary coins. It was impossible, it was contended, or ridiculously inconvenient, to make gold coins small enough for use in the millions of necessary small transactions, like buying a newspaper or a loaf of bread. What was needed was a subsidiary coinage, which represented halves, quarters, tenths, or hundredths of the standard unit. These coins, regardless of what they were made of, or what their intrinsic value might be, would be legally acceptable and convertible, at the rates stamped on them, into the standard gold coins.

It would be very difficult, I admit, to provide for this with a purely private currency, with everybody having the legal power to stamp out his own coins and guarantee their conversion by him into gold. It is clear, in short, that a government-provided or a government-regulated coinage has some advantages. But these advantages are bought at a price. That price seemed comparatively low in the nineteenth century and until 1914, but today the price of government control of money has become exorbitant practically everywhere.

The basic problem that confronts us is not one that is confined to the monetary sphere. It is a problem of government. It is in fact *the* problem of government in every sphere. We need government to prevent or minimize internal and external violence and aggression and to keep the peace. But we are obliged to recognize that no group of men can be completely trusted with power. All power is liable to be abused, and the greater the power the greater the likelihood of abuse. For that reason only minimum powers should be granted to government. But the tendency of government everywhere has been to use even minimum powers to increase its powers. And any government is certain to use great powers to usurp still greater powers. There is no doubt that the two great world wars since 1914 brought on the present prevalence of the quasi-omnipotent State.

But the solution of the overall problem of government is beyond the province of this book. To decide what would be the best obtainable monetary system, if we could get it, would be a sufficiently formidable problem in itself. But a major part of the solution to this problem, to repeat once more, will be *how to get the monetary system out of the hands of the politicians.* Certainly as long as we retain our nearly omnipotent redistributive State, no sound currency will be possible.

178

24

Free Choice of Currencies

The preceding chapter originally appeared, in slightly different form, in the *Freeman* of November 1975 (Foundation for Economic Education, Irvington-on-Hudson, N.Y.). Since then, Professor F. A. Hayek, the Nobel laureate, has published two remarkable pamphlets embodying similar proposals, but carrying them in some important respects further.

The first of these is *Choice in Currency*.[1] I find this wholly admirable. Hayek begins by pointing out that the chief root of our recent monetary troubles is the scientific authority which the Keynesians seemed to give to the superstition that increasing the quantity of money can ensure prosperity and full employment. He then proceeds to point out the fallacies in this view. Inflation, however, he concedes, even before explicit Keynesianism, largely dominated monetary history until the emergence of the gold standard. The gold standard brought two centuries of relatively stable prices and made possible the development of modern industrialism: "It was the main function of the gold standard, of balanced budgets, of the necessity for deficit countries to contract their circulation, and of the limitation of the supply of 'international liquidity,' " he

---

[1] London: The Institute of Economic Affairs, 1976.

179

points out, "to make it impossible for the monetary authorities to capitulate to the pressure for more money."[2]

But under present world political conditions he does not believe that we can now remedy the situation by

> *constructing* some new international monetary order, whether a new international monetary authority or institution, or even an international agreement to adopt a particular mechanism or system of policy, such as the classical gold standard. I am fairly convinced that any attempt now to re-instate the gold standard by international agreement would break down within a short time and merely discredit the ideal of an international gold standard for even longer. Without the conviction of the public at large that certain immediately painful measures are occasionally necessary to preserve reasonable stability, we cannot hope that any authority which has the power to determine the quantity of money will long resist the pressure for, or the seduction of, cheap money.[3]

What, then, is the remedy? What is so dangerous and ought to be done away with, Hayek insists, is not the right of governments to issue money but their *exclusive* right to do so and their power to force people to use it and to accept it at a particular price. The legal tender laws should be repealed.

A great deal of confusion has existed about this. It is necessary, of course, for the government to decide what kind of money it will accept in payment of taxes, and it is necessary for the courts to be able to decide, in case of dispute, in what kind of money private debts should be paid. No doubt, in the absence of specification, courts would continue to decide that debts can be paid off in the official money of the country, no matter how much it may have depreciated. But if the debtor and creditor have expressly contracted for a payment to be made in gold, or in Swiss francs, or in German marks, then the courts should hold that contract valid. The common law of enforcement of contracts should apply.

---

[2] *Choice in Currency*, p. 15.
[3] *Ibid.*

The immediate advantages of this should be obvious. A government would no longer be able to protect its money against competition. If it continued to inflate, its citizens would forsake its money for other currencies. Inflation would no longer pay.

There is, in a sense, nothing novel about Hayek's proposal. Toward the end of the German hyperinflation of 1919–23, people refused to accept the old paper marks on any terms, and began to do business with each other in gold, dollars, Swiss francs, and even in a multitude of private currencies. But in any country in which the legal tender laws did not exist, inflation would never again go to such tragic lengths, if, indeed, it could be continued to any substantial extent at all.

If the present writer were to venture a prediction, it would be that when the gold standard is restored—as I believe it eventually will be—it is far more likely to be restored first, not in countries that have been suffering the least, but in those that have been suffering the most inflation. It will first happen, not by deliberate governmental policy, but by breakdown and default. No matter what the nominal legal penalties, people will cease doing business in the national paper money. (They did so not only in Germany in 1923, but in the assignat period in France, and in Soviet Russia in 1923.)

De-Monopolization of Money

I should like to turn now to the second Hayek pamphlet that I referred to a few pages back. This is called *Denationalization of Money*.[4]

It followed eights months after *Choice in Currency*, and it continues the argument put forward in the latter. That argument is summarized in ten numbered points printed on the pamphlet's back cover. I quote the first five:

> 1. The government monopoly of money must be abolished to stop the recurring bouts of acute inflation and deflation that have become accentuated during the last 60 years.

---

[4] London: The Institute of Economic Affairs, 1976.

2. Abolition is also the cure for the more deep-seated disease of the recurring waves of depression and unemployment attributed to "capitalism."

3. The monopoly of money by government has relieved it of the need to keep its expenditure within its revenue and has thus precipitated the spectacular increase in government expenditure over the last thirty years.

4. Abolition of the monopoly of money would make it increasingly impossible for governments to restrict the international movement of men, money and capital that safeguard the ability of dissidents to escape oppression.

5. These four defects—inflation, instability, undisciplined state expenditure, economic nationalization—have a common origin and a common cure: the replacement of the governmert monopoly of money by competition in currency supplied by private issuers who, to preserve public confidence, will limit the quantity of their paper issue and thus maintain its value. This is the "denationalization" of money.

Most libertarians can endorse the first four of these points unreservedly. About the fifth and those following I personally harbor grave doubts.

"Free" private currencies have been tried. In our early American history they were tried repeatedly in nearly all the existing states. Some of the states issued their own "legal-tender" money, usually with disastrous results; and most of the private currencies that they licensed met with little better fate. Panics and financial collapses became a matter of course. To take one state at random, in Michigan, after 1836:

> Fraudulent overissues were frequent and in many cases not even recorded. Before long a million dollars in worthless bank notes were in circulation, a bewildering variety of issues each circulating at its own rate of discount with a confusion that required corps of bookkeepers to keep the accounts of a firm straight. Merchants kept couriers by whom they hurried off to

the banks the notes they were compelled to take, in order to exchange them—if possible—for something which had more value. Misery and bankruptcy spread over the state. . . . The climax came in 1844 when, nearly all the "free banks" being in the hands of receivers, the state supreme court held that the general banking law had been passed in violation of the constitution and hence that even the receiverships had no legal existence![5]

Other states made other provisions and other reserve requirements for note issues by private banks, but the history of laxly controlled private-note issue in all the states is depressingly similar. The interested reader can find a short but excellent account in Groseclose's *Money and Man* (pp. 180–93).

In the light of this history, I can only regard with astonishment the extraordinary optimism of Hayek regarding the outcome of unrestricted private-note issue. He assures us that private competition in issuing money will lead us to a far sounder money than the classical gold standard was ever able to provide. The private issuers, he seems to assume, will in all cases be scrupulously honest, and will have in mind only their long-run self-interest; and therefore *"money is the one thing competition would not make cheap, because its attractiveness rests on its preserving its 'dearness'"* (italics in original).[6]

Hayek does not seem to think that it is either necessary or desirable for the private issuers of currency to keep it convertible into gold. He suggests that their money could consist of "different abstract units."[7] How a currency could consist of a merely "abstract" unit, and how a private issuer could get it launched and accepted at a "precisely defined"[8] purchasing power, he does not explain.

If he were in charge of one of the major Swiss joint-stock banks, he tells us, he would issue a unit called, say, a "ducat." "And I would announce that I proposed from time to time to state the

[5] Elgin Groseclose, *Money and Man,* 4th ed. (Norman, Okla.: University of Oklahoma Press, 1976), p. 188.

[6] *Denationalization of Money,* p. 74

[7] *Ibid.,* p. 25.

[8] *Ibid.,* p. 39.

precise commodity equivalent in terms of which I intended to keep the value of the ducat constant, but that I reserved the right, after announcement, to alter the composition of the commodity standard as experience and the revealed preferences of the public suggested."[9]

It is clear that Hayek has in mind that private issuers could and should adopt a "commodity reserve," or "market basket," standard. (He has advocated such a standard for a long time. For example, in *The Constitution of Liberty,* he tells us: "A commodity reserve standard which has been worked out in some detail appears to me still the best plan for achieving all the advantages attributed to the gold standard without its defects."[10] And he refers there to an essay advocating such a currency that he published as early as 1943.)

But Hayek is bafflingly vague concerning how a private issuer would maintain the value or purchasing power of such a currency. He says that "the issuing institution could achieve this result by regulating the quantity of its issue" (p. 43) and by keeping it "scarce" (p. 85). But quantity and scarcity mean nothing in this context except in relation to the liquid assets of the particular issuer and his demonstrated ability and readiness to keep his currency unit convertible on demand into the precise weight of the concrete commodity that his unit is supposed to be worth. He can make it convertible into a gram of gold or an ounce of silver or a pound of tobacco or a bushel of wheat. But there is no feasible way in which he could make it convertible into, say, a specified amount of each of the 400 or so commodities and services that enter into the official consumer price index, not to speak of the 2,700 commodities in the official wholesale price index. And no holder of his currency would in any case want to load himself down with these and give himself the problem of disposing of them.[11]

---

[9] *Ibid.*

[10] Chicago: University of Chicago Press, 1960, p. 335.

[11] In the 1943 essay by Hayek that I previously mentioned, "A Commodity Reserve Currency," included in his *Individualism and Economic Order* (Chicago: University of Chicago Press, 1948), he endorses a scheme by Benjamin Graham involving only twenty-four different commodities. I need not discuss that plan in detail here, and will say only that I regard it as incredibly clumsy, complicated, costly, wasteful, unsettling, and altogether impracticable. It was in any case proposed as a government scheme, and would inevitably have become a political football.

I confess myself unable to follow the assumptions behind Hayek's currency proposal. A long-established government money has an established purchasing power, even though additional paper-money issues reduce it. But how does a private issuer establish the value of his money unit in the first place? Why would anybody take it? Who would accept his certificates for their own goods or services? And at what rate? Against *what* would the private banker issue his money? With *what* would the would-be user buy it from him? Into *what* would the issuer keep it constantly convertible? These are the essential questions.

To assure a dependable, definite, and precise value for anything in terms of anything else, the first must be constantly convertible into the second. Under a gold standard each currency unit is constantly convertible, on demand, into a precise weight of gold. This not only assures a precise value for the pound, for example, and a precise value for the dollar; it also assures a precise "parity" ratio between the pound and the dollar, or any other two currencies. Of course it is possible to suspend gold convertibility and continue to maintain a fixed parity rate between the pound and the dollar by making them freely convertible into each other at that rate. For a time this was actually done (sometimes by government-pegging operations, which amounted to nearly the same thing).

But you cannot make a currency convertible into an abstraction. You cannot make a currency convertible into an index number. A true "commodity" dollar or ducat would have to be convertible into a precise quantity of each of a thousand different commodities. A private issuer cannot assure any specific or definite value for his money unit by limiting the volume of its issuance. There is no fixed and dependable relationship or ratio between the two. The crucial question in the mind of the holder, or the accepter, will always be: What can I be *confident* of getting in exchange for this?

Others before Hayek have had a similar yearning for a commodity standard, but have been aware of this practical problem. The most prominent is Irving Fisher, who in the 1920s proposed his "compensated dollar." This is a dollar that would have been convertible into a constantly changing quantity of gold, to keep it fixed in value in relation to an average price of commodities as determined by an official index.

Fisher's compensated gold dollar would have solved the problem of the utter impracticability of any direct conversion of a currency unit into a trainload or shipload of assorted commodities, but it would have solved it at a prohibitive cost. As Benjamin M. Anderson[12] and others pointed out, it would have enabled international speculators to speculate with impunity against the dollar and the American gold reserve, and would have had other self-defeating and confidence-undermining effects.

What is strangest about the fascination that a commodity, or "fixed-purchasing-power," standard has exercized over some otherwise brilliant minds is that such a standard is quite unnecessary. As Murray N. Rothbard has put it: "If creditors and debtors want to hedge against future changes in purchasing power, they can do so easily on the free market. When they make their contracts, they can agree that repayment will be made in a sum of money *adjusted* by some agreed-upon index number of changes in the value of money." [13]

Since the foregoing criticism of Hayek's proposal was written, a new and enlarged edition of Hayek's pamphlet has appeared.[14] It contains many additional true and penetrating observations, but nothing to answer the objections to the particular kind of private currencies he envisions. He rejects a sound, historically tested basis of money to embrace a visionary one. Some of his arguments take one's breath away. For example: "The value of a currency redeemable in gold is not *derived* [his italics] from the value of that gold, but merely kept at the same value through the automatic regulation of its quantity" (p. 105). This is something like saying that the value of a warehouse receipt is not determined by the value of the goods to which it acknowledges legal title, but simply by the total number of warehouse receipts.

Hayek recognizes that the type of private paper money he recommends would be "a mere token money" (p. 108), redeemable in nothing and convertible into nothing—not even into the huge miscellany of commodities in terms of which its value is supposedly stablized. But he still expects people to accept it in exchange for their own labor or goods, and at the value that the issuer says it has. There is no reason to suppose that anybody would so accept

---

[12] See his *Economics and the Public Welfare* (New York: Van Nostrand, 1949), ch. 51.

[13] Murray N. Rothbard, *What Has Government Done to Our Money?*, 2nd ed. (Santa Ana, Calif.: Rampart College 1974), p. 17.

[14] *Denationalization of Money*, 2nd ed. (London: The Institute of Economic Affairs, 1978).

it. This "commodity reserve" money is a dream-world currency. It would consist of private non-interest-bearing perpetually outstanding promissory notes saying, in effect, "I owe you nothing."

For a Private Gold Standard

This whole discussion of a private commodity-reserve currency may seem like a diversion which I could have avoided. I have made it chiefly because Hayek's deservedly great authority might otherwise lead some persons to advocate a false remedy and others to reject the whole idea of a private currency as chimerical.

But we can safely return to the recommendations of Hayek's earlier pamphlet of 1976, *Choice in Currency,* and to my own suggestion of a private gold standard in 1975. Both are entirely valid.

Let us not reject the gold standard because governments once embraced it. After all, it was the end-product of centuries of experience. It was the survival of the fittest against the early competition of oxen, sheep, hides, wampum, tobacco, iron, copper, bronze, and finally of silver. It was the outcome of competition in the market place, as I am confident it would be again. It was only after its victory in private use that governments took it over, exploited it for their own purposes, diluted it, perverted it, and finally destroyed it.

Let us see where this leads us: Governments should be deprived of their monopoly of the currency-issuing power. The private citizens of every country should be allowed, by mutual agreement, to do business with each other in the currency of any other country. In addition, they should be allowed to mint privately gold or silver coins and to do business with each other in such coins. (Each coin should bear the stamp, trademark, or emblem of its coiner and specify its exact round weight—one gram, ten grams, or whatever. It would be preferably referred to by that weight—a "goldgram," say, and not bear any more abstract name like dollar or ducat.) Still further, private institutions should be allowed to issue notes payable in such metals. But these should be only gold or silver certificates, redeemable on demand in the respective quantities of the metals specified. The issuers should be required to hold at all times the full amount in metal of the notes they have issued, as a warehouse owner is required to hold at all times everything against which he has issued an outstanding warehouse receipt, on penalty of being prosecuted for fraud. And the courts should enforce all contracts made in good faith in such private currencies.

At first glance this proposal would seem to be much more restrictive and hampering than the Hayek scheme. But any law permitting private currencies, it seems to me, should provide safeguards to minimize loss to holders, and a definitely ascertainable liability of the issuer for misrepresentation, fraud, breach of contract, or default. This is what my suggested limitations are designed to make possible.

My proposal would, in fact—if it could be achieved—lead to an almost revolutionary monetary reform. The competition of foreign currencies and of private coins and certificates would bring almost immediate improvement in most national currencies. The governments would have to slow down or halt their inflations to get their own citizens to continue to use their government's money in preference to the most attractive foreign currencies, or to private gold or silver certificates.

But something far more important would happen. As the use of the private currencies expanded, a private gold standard would develop. And because of the restrictions placed on it, it would be a pure, a 100 percent, gold standard. The government fractional-reserve gold standard—which was the classical gold standard—was finally strectched and abused to the point where, in my opinion, it can never be restored by any single nation or even by a "world authority."

But this, when one comes to think of it, will be ultimately a tremendous boon. For though people will probably again never trust a fractional-reserve gold standard, they *will* trust a full gold standard. And they will trust it the more if it is no longer in the exclusive custody of governments, consisting of vote-seeking politicians and bureaucrats, but in private custody. The gold reserves will no longer be held solely in huge national piles subject often to the overnight whim or ukase of a single man (a Franklin Roosevelt or a Richard Nixon). Gold coins will circulate, and be held by millions, and the gold reserves will be distributed among thousands of private vaults. The private certificate-issuers would not be allowed to treat this gold held in trust—as governments have—as if it had somehow become their own property. (Central banks, and in the U.S. that engine of inflation known as the Federal Reserve System, would of course be abolished.)

I should like to point out here that my proposal of private gold coinage is not, like Dr. Hayek's price-index money, untried or utopian, but merely suggests the restoration of a right previously exercised in American history. Our Constitution provides, in Article I, Section 8, that: "The Congress shall have the power to ... coin money" and "regulate the value thereof." In Section 10 of the same article it provides that: "No State shall ... coin money." But it does not prohibit individuals from doing so.

As early as 1840 the director of the mint, in his report to Congress, referred to one C. Bechtler, who operated a private mint in Rutherfordton, North Carolina, in competition with the U.S. mint at Charlotte. The mint director complained that he could take no legal action against Bechtler: "It seems strange that the privilege of coinage should be carefully confined by law to the General Government, while that of coining gold and silver, though withheld from the States, is freely permitted to individuals, with the single restriction that they must not imitate the coinage established by law."[15]

Gold was discovered in California in January 1848, more than two years before California was accepted as a state. Private issues of gold coins and ingots were the dominant media of exchange in the state until at least 1855. Bank notes did not circulate there until quite late. During the federal issuance of greenbacks during the Civil War, the California state legislature passed, and the state courts enforced, the Specific Performance Act, or Specific Contract Law (April 27, 1863). This provided that if a contract specifically provided that a debt was to be repaid in gold coin, it must be paid in gold coin, not in paper. Between 1860 and 1862, private gold coins continued to be minted in Denver. The federal government had to buy the mint out in 1863. It was not until an act of Congress on June 8, 1864, that private coinage was prohibited.[16]

I should perhaps make one point clear. I do not expect that allowing citizens to do business in the currencies of foreign nations or in private gold coins will in the long run in most countries mean that these citizens will do most of their business in these foreign or private currencies. I am assuming that practically all governments will continue to issue an official currency and that, when they have ceased inflating, they will issue their own gold coins and

---

[15] E. H. Adams, *Private Gold Coinage of California, 1849–1855*, 1975, p. xi.

[16] For a more detailed account, see Carl Watner, "California Gold, 1849–65," *Reason*, January 1976.

certificates. And I assume that most of their citizens will then use their own governments' money and coins. But this is because I expect that once freedom of choice in currencies is permitted, each government will begin to reform its own monetary practices. What will count is not only the *actual* competition of foreign money or private coins, but the ever-present *possibility* of the competition of foreign or private money. What is chiefly necessary, in brief, is to break the government monopoly of money issuance. When that is done, reform will follow.

Permitting private gold coinage and private gold-certificate issues will allow us to bring the world back to a pure gold standard. This has hitherto been considered an utterly hopeless project. As long as we were operating on a fractional-reserve gold standard, any attempt to return to a pure, or 100 percent, gold standard would have involved a devastating deflation, a ruinous fall of prices. But now that not only the United States, but every other nation, has abandoned a gold standard completely, the former problem no longer exists. The beginning of the new reform would bring a dual or parallel system of prices—prices in gold, and prices in the outstanding government paper money. In the transition period, prices would be stated in both currencies, until the government paper money either became worthless, or the issuing government itself returned to a gold standard and accepted its outstanding paper issues at a fixed conversion rate. (An example of this was the German government's acceptance of a trillion old paper marks for a new rentenmark—and finally a gold mark—after 1923.)

Government-issued money did supply a uniform subsidiary coinage. It is hard (though not impossible) to see how a private currency could solve this problem satisfactorily. Perhaps governments could be trusted to continue to mint a uniform subsidiary coinage and keep a 100 percent gold reserve at least against this.

But apart from such comparatively minor problems, I can see no great difficulties in the way of a private money. The main problem is not economic; it is political. It is how to get governments voluntarily to repeal their legal tender laws and to surrender their monopoly of money issue. I confess I cannot see precisely how this political problem is going to be solved. But it is the urgent and immediate goal to which every citizen who can recognize the great jeopardy in which we all stand should now direct his efforts.

Index of Names